W9-CCW-384

ELEMENTARY
SCHOOL
TEACHING

Problems and Methods

Goodyear Education Series

Theodore W. Hipple, *Editor*
UNIVERSITY OF FLORIDA

ELEMENTARY SCHOOL TEACHING: PROBLEMS AND METHODS
MARGARET KELLY GIBLIN

POPULAR MEDIA AND THE TEACHING OF ENGLISH
THOMAS R. GIBLIN

SCHOOL COUNSELING: PROBLEMS AND METHODS
ROBERT MYRICK and JOE WITTMER

SECONDARY SCHOOL COUNSELING: PROBLEMS AND METHODS
THEODORE W. HIPPLE

WILL THE REAL TEACHER PLEASE STAND UP?
A PRIMER IN HUMANISTIC EDUCATION
MARY GREER and BONNIE RUBINSTEIN

ELEMENTARY SCHOOL TEACHING
Problems and Methods

Margaret Kelly Giblin

83062

LIBRARY

GOODYEAR PUBLISHING COMPANY, INC.

Pacific Palisades, California

Copyright © 1972 by GOODYEAR PUBLISHING COMPANY, Inc.
Pacific Palisades, California

All rights reserved. No part of this book may be reproduced in any
form or by any means without permission in writing from the
publisher.

Y-2717-0

ISBN: 0-87620-271-7

Library of Congress Catalog Card Number: 77-188278

Current printing (last number):
10 9 8 7 6 5 4 3 2 1

Printed in the United States of America

LB
1555
G53

PREFACE

Intended for instruction of pre-service teachers and relatively inexperienced in-service teachers, this book is designed for active participation in the problems encountered by elementary and middle-school teachers. The problems incorporate experiences in problem solving, value clarification, and decision making that teachers face daily. They are extracted from real teaching incidents.

There are two premises underlying this book. The first is that most teacher dissatisfaction, anxiety, and frustration stem from difficulties in human relations and teaching strategy, not a deficiency in subject preparation. Frequently a teacher feels ineffectual because he cannot maintain class control or because he cannot establish satisfactory interactions with his colleagues. Self-confidence is exceedingly important in achieving teaching success and happiness. It is hoped that discussion and other activities derived from the study of these problems will increase an individual's confidence and ability to cope with these situations.

The second assumption is that learning, to be effective, must be personally meaningful. The theory-practice bond is strengthened when opportunities are provided for application and integration of theoretical concepts. Teachers need more extensive experiences in education than universities and communities can, or will, provide. To date, field experiences have not been so diversified as to include varying socio-economic conditions, faculty organizations, curricular and instructional designs, or other complexities of a teacher's role. Novice teachers can grow professionally through explorations of the problems encountered by their colleagues. This book is mainly composed of such problems, and the format of their presentation virtually demands reader participation. Moreover, the problems included in the text are drawn from general areas of teaching relationships and procedures; they are not specifically subject matter in nature.

Each case is actually a four-page unit, with a statement of the problem on the initial page, a blank facing page on which the reader can write how he would solve the problem and why he thinks his solution would be effective, a third page—again blank—on which the reader can write his reactions to the alternate solutions, presented to him on the fourth page. These solutions are given in no particular order; they are listed randomly to encourage reader attention to all of them.

Following the collection of problems on each topic is a brief overview of that topic. This overview is not intended to be a comprehensive statement. Rather it is direct, sometimes blunt, advice, especially designed for the future teacher who has more questions than answers: How do you encourage student self-discipline? What must be considered when you individualize instruction? How do you measure student progress?

Finally, a short bibliography completes each chapter so that the reader who is anxious to further explore some of the topics has an opportunity to secure additional and, not infrequently, different perspectives and suggestions. The bibliographic entries, in many instances, are appropriate for several topics.

The arrangement of topics or sequence of problems is not meant to imply a hierarchy of importance. Each reader is as unique as the students he will teach. One new teacher might anticipate with anxiety meeting parents, while another might primarily fear meeting his colleagues and principal. No less a problem than the order of sections is their interrelatedness. The topics and their problems are inherently interwoven into a total educational scene. It is only for purposes of easy examination of each that they are presented in isolation.

The problems, though, make the book. In addition to the universal problems of reporting pupil progress and establishing a learning climate are instances concerning bilingual cultures, drug culture, and integration. They deal with the feelings and attitudes of teachers. The problems of individualizing instruction seem appropriate as a focal point, whether the situation is urban, suburban, rural, self-contained, teamed, departmentalized, graded, or nongraded. With all of these problems, teachers can come to grips, if only vicariously, with circumstances they may eventually confront. Providing their own solutions, they can compare reactions and justifications with their colleagues. Out of such activity can come, I believe, teachers who are better able to face themselves and cope with the problems they will encounter in the process of becoming a teacher. If they are more secure, confident, and effective teachers as a result of integrating the study of these problems into their personal experiences, then their time in reading this book and my time in writing it will have been worthwhile.

I wish to clarify one issue that deeply concerned me while selecting these problems. It must be continually remembered that this book is centered around difficulties teachers face. Such a concentration of problems must be perceived in a proper perspective. Teaching is one of the most challenging, stimulating, creative, enjoyable activities I know. Its joys and satisfactions are limitless and must not be overlooked.

There are many to whom I owe thanks for contributing to this volume. Credit is certainly due two groups of learners: many elementary school children who, with much patience, taught me many things; and University of Florida undergraduates who deepened my sensitivities about the teaching-learning continuum. In addition, I owe a great deal to my New York and Florida colleagues for their contributions. I am indebted to Charles Christmann and H. Edward Litteer, who provided encouragement and guidance, perfectly timed, in my growth in becoming a teacher. Asahel Woodruff and Art Combs had a great deal of influence in shaping my teaching philosophy and practices. Indeed, I am grateful to Ted Hipple, author of *Secondary School Teaching: Problems and Methods,* for providing the opportunity, impetus, and encouragement for this venture.

There are three very special "thank yous" to convey. The first and second are extended to my parents who are intuitively very fine teachers. The third is reserved for my husband, Tom, whose understanding and responsiveness have kept me in a constant state of "becoming a teacher."

CONTENTS

ELEMENTARY
SCHOOL
TEACHING

Problems and Methods

CHAPTER ONE

Pupil-Teacher Relationships

DANGEROUS DONALD

Donald is an only child in a broken marriage and is now living with his grandparents; his cumulative folder reflects his "need for attention," which you determine—after two months—is an understatement! He monopolizes all group discussions, diverts small group attention with his jokes and science fiction stories, provokes his neighbors, and delights in producing field mice and garter snakes at well-chosen moments. Realizing that the bigger his audience, the better he performs, and having exhausted the solutions provided in your Educational Psychology notes, you finally begin a campaign for Donald's classmates to ignore his behavior. With Donald present, the class discusses ways to "help" him and decides that the best way is to pretend he isn't present when he carries on his antics—unless it's an appropriate time, such as "free time" or playground recess.

Initially you are relieved because it appears the classroom strategy is going to be effective, but one Monday morning the principal catches him inserting bobby pins in an electrical outlet in the corridor. You have a three-way heart-to-heart talk about your concerns for his safety, emphasizing how well you like him and how the children look to him for leadership and comic relief. Much to your amazement, he responds passively for the remainder of the day and most of Tuesday until he begins to "cut-up" again in Music. The music teacher reprimands his behavior by sending him to sit outside her closed door and discovers him missing at the end of her class. After a frantic search of the school, he is found in the faculty parking lot, lying under *your* car!

The new ways Donald has invented to get attention are jeopardizing his welfare as well as inching you closer to that nervous breakdown you're convinced you're about to have. You decide that some immediate action must be taken.

YOUR SOLUTION

YOUR REACTIONS TO THE ALTERNATE SOLUTIONS

ALTERNATE SOLUTIONS

1. Revise your classroom strategy and get the cooperation of the special teachers.

2. Suspend or expell Donald on the grounds that his behavior is unsuitable for public school.

3. Refer his case to the social worker with the recommendation that he should be placed in a foster home.

4. Give him the benefit of the doubt and suggest that he should be assigned to another teacher to ensure him a "fresh" start.

5. Recommend him for placement in a class for the emotionally disturbed.

6. Visit a psychiatrist yourself.

IN SEARCH OF ACCEPTANCE . . .

A discipline problem Steven is not; in fact, you wish he would assert himself in social interactions for he is never angered and is easily swayed by his peers in his search for acceptance. Steven is spending his second year in grade 4 and so is challenged to cope with all the stigma of a "repeater." Despite your attempts to individualize his curriculum and to provide him with success, his classmates only believe Steven is bigger and dumber than they are and openly resent your praise of his positive contributions.

Saved or stifled by his sense of humor, Steven readily accepts blame whether or not he is responsible; he pulls practical jokes others who wouldn't dare to convince him to do; he deliberately loses individual competitions when he thinks it will please his latest friend. In sum, he's everyone's favorite patsy and for weeks you've been contemplating the best way to help him.

Your temper boils when he accepts the responsibility for urinating on the lavatory ceiling and walls the past three days during "free time." Nearly simultaneous with a classmate's announcement of this reoccurrence, Steven darts to your side. In full view of his classmates, Steven chokes and sobs his confession and vows never to do it again.

His dramatic, convincing performance could have won him an Oscar but you know he is not the culprit. In his eagerness to accept the blame once again, Steven has forgotten he spent the last three periods of "free time" unpacking new books in the media center.

YOUR SOLUTION

YOUR REACTIONS TO THE ALTERNATE SOLUTIONS

ALTERNATE SOLUTIONS

1. Confront Steven with the fact that he was in the media center all three days and see how he reacts.
2. Continue to accept his confessions and reprimand him, as you haven't decided yet how to "help" him.
3. Have him psychoanalyzed because of his desire for punishment.
4. Initiate a sign-up sheet for using the lavatory.
5. Ask him to clean the lavatory.

LACKADAISICAL LAURENCE

"I'm not overweight. I'm just five inches too short!"

Laurence's self-description gives you some insight into his personality. He has a keen sense of humor and is invariably seen meandering about your classroom, hands in pockets, unhurried, calm, and easygoing in all circumstances. Laurence loves to shuffle from one place to another engaging anyone and everyone in conversation. He is well liked by his peers.

Although you have been in this student teaching situation only several hours, Laurence's patterns of academic behavior are beginning to concern you. He appears lazy! In a structured setting where everyone does the same assignment, he listens attentively to the task description and once everyone has begun he quietly says, "I don't want to do that, and besides you don't want to see the same thing thirty times; I'll just not do mine and save you all that work." In independent or small-group activities, he wanders around reviewing and listening to the work of others and returns to you whispering, "I really don't want to do this just now, but if I can make a suggestion, wouldn't it be easier if you . . ." Even during free time when he can choose anything to do he continues his visitations.

As a personal challenge you determine to change Laurence's attitude and behavior toward academics. Selecting the direct approach in a conversation with him, you ask why he never completes academic assignments and why he prefers to spend his time socializing. He responds, "Oh, don't worry about me. Worrying causes mental illness! Do you know that teachers as a group have a high percentage of mental illness?" Chuckling to himself as he walks away, he adds, "You're too nice to have that happen to you!"

Now, more baffled than before, you are really going to have to interest Laurence in pursuing educational requirements and to help him develop effective study skills.

Where will you begin?

YOUR SOLUTION

YOUR REACTIONS TO THE ALTERNATE SOLUTIONS

ALTERNATE SOLUTIONS

1. With your cooperating teacher and college coordinator, explore various methods of motivating Laurence.

2. Loan a cassette tape recorder to Laurence for the day so he can more effectively review how he spends his time; then make suggestions for improvement.

3. Invest in a model rocket, begin assembling it, and hope that it interests Laurence enough to get him partially or totally involved in its completion.

4. Pupil team him with a domineering, conscientious student who will insist upon Laurence's help in finishing the task.

5. Capitalize on Laurence's verbal ability by giving him a lead role in a dramatic production.

6. Leave him be, confident that eventually something will captivate his attention.

PRESCRIPTION FOR TRUDY?

You are surprised your first day of teaching when Trudy, a lovely girl with a cherubic smile, has expended your patience and challenged your teaching skills. A quick glance through her cumulative folder reveals her apparent potential but also reports four years of labels such as "hyperactive," "emotionally disturbed," "socially maladjusted," and "nonreader."

The second day of school Trudy's parents request a conference with you, which is immediately arranged. Rumors report that the parents are highly qualified, renowned Child physicians—one in psychology. Meeting with them you realize that both value intellectual achievement and will do anything to get their children to reach it. You are warned to "guard Trudy every moment and strictly discipline her when her mind wanders from her studies." Amidst bickering between themselves about who should shoulder the blame for Trudy's lack of achievement and misconduct, you receive the impression that Trudy is considered the source of all family misfortunes. They have moved three times due to "neighborhood pressures" created by Trudy. Additionally, aggravation persists between Trudy and her brother because his playmates are forbidden to play with "Trudy's brother."

Wrapping up their forty-minute dialogue, Trudy's parents return to their reason for the conference. After extensive private testing and continued mental duress, they are recommending that Trudy take a stimulant in pill form; it is, as yet, an experimental medication but claims to date have shown that it can calm the hyperactive child, making her more cooperative and extending her attention span. They propose that this may be an avenue to helping Trudy achieve her academic potential, but they want your professional opinion.

What is your answer?

YOUR SOLUTION

YOUR REACTIONS TO THE ALTERNATE SOLUTIONS

ALTERNATE SOLUTIONS

1. In the interest of Trudy's welfare, report that she has already shown signs of independence, self-discipline, and promise of solving some of her own problems, so you would prefer delaying action on their recommendation.

2. Confront Trudy's parents with the possibility that they might be contributing to, if not causing, her emotional and academic difficulties.

3. On a trial basis only, approve the drug prescription.

4. Agree with her parents that stimulants for hyperactive children may have advantages; however, the research you've read proves that learning decreases ultimately; therefore, you tell them you will not endorse their recommendation.

5. Suggest that perhaps a better solution for Trudy and her family is to temporarily place her in a foster home.

6. Agree with their recommendation on the basis that because of their backgrounds and your limited experiences with Trudy they are in the best position to make this decision.

GUILTY UNTIL PROVEN INNOCENT

Juanita is your new pupil who speaks all too little English, as she moved from Cuba just two days ago. Although not long ago you were president of your high-school Spanish Club, you're embarrassed that the only Spanish you recall is "Buenos dias" to welcome her. Your tension is eased by Juanita's new classmates who usher her through the daily activities. Not only is she the center of attention, but by dismissal time she leaves school with several suitors trailing close behind. Language is certainly no barrier for these students!

Rummaging through your dusty school books at home, you spy with relief your Spanish dictionary and refer to it while making Spanish and English cards naming objects around the classroom. Making the best of this situation, you plan for everyone to learn some conversation in a second language and are enthusiastic about prospective language-learning possibilities.

Your pupils are eager to become "bilinguists" until several weeks after Juanita's arrival when small, inexpensive items are mysteriously disappearing daily from pupils' desks, lunchboxes, and jackets. A child discovers your cherished storybook and two favorite games missing, and you try to nonchalantly reply that they must be misplaced. The children, however, have their own theories, which are mirrored in their behavior. Groans are their responses to language period, and Juanita is socially isolated and ignored. No longer is she demanded as a lunch partner, game participant, or teammate! She is the accused thief! After several days of their silent treatment, Juanita is no longer able to contain her feelings, for she bursts into tears and runs out the door. Finding her just outside, you give her a chance to compose herself whereupon you re-enter the ever-so-quiet classroom together.

Juanita returns to her seat. Meanwhile, your class is waiting!

YOUR SOLUTION

YOUR REACTIONS TO THE ALTERNATE SOLUTIONS

ALTERNATE SOLUTIONS

1. Ask your class to explain the reason for their behavior. Examine it for fact and supposition.

2. Role-play the parts of several students and Juanita to explore involved feelings.

3. Discuss the nature of items missing to determine why anyone might want them and where one might hide them.

4. Suggest that the pupils have developed an unfounded conclusion about Juanita and that you want all the "borrowed" things returned by tomorrow night.

5. Brainstorm reasons why anyone would benefit by blaming Juanita for the robberies and discuss alternative solutions for a person to follow.

CYNTHIA'S ESCAPADES

The jokes in the faculty lounge about the stampede and trampling of bus duty weren't as exaggerated as you'd thought. The arch of your foot is already black-and-blue and your shoes are scuffed after the first bus unloads. You laugh out loud as you think of how your image will be after the twentieth bus! This is your first day of bus duty, fifth week of teaching.

As the pupils descend from the school bus, you can't help but notice Cynthia, one of your students, who is usually well dressed and groomed. This morning she looks disheveled and carries her shoes in her hand. Just as she heads into school her eyes roll and she begins vomiting. Helping you to get Cynthia to the nurse's office, the bus driver describes Cynthia's irrational behavior on the bus and implies that the "usual gent" waited with her until the bus came to meet her. With the nurse's arrival you learn that Cynthia has been rumored living with a man and that she's openly boasted easy access to the drug culture.

An ambulance arrives, whisking the building principal and Cynthia to the hospital, where she claims to have swallowed a large quantity of aspirin. The librarian covers your class while you call Cynthia's mother to explain the situation. Outwardly irritated by your call, her mother informs you that she wants no part of Cynthia's troubles and that the juvenile shelter, "although too good for her," is the place to call. She hangs up. You dial the number again but there is no answer. You return to your eleven-year-olds and your teaching responsibility, having requested that any news from the hospital be relayed to you. The children are uneasy and curious. What happened to Cynthia? Where did she go? When will she be back? Is she going to be all right? You give brief but honest answers.

As things begin to settle down, Cynthia, barefoot and breathless, enters the room announcing her escape from the principal and hospital attendants. Your move.

YOUR SOLUTION

YOUR REACTIONS TO THE ALTERNATE SOLUTIONS

ALTERNATE SOLUTIONS

1. Welcome her back and invite her to join in her classmates' activities.

2. Tell her to meet you in the principal's office where you will again try to reach her mother by phone.

3. Coax Cynthia into group projects and call the juvenile shelter in addition to the hospital.

4. Suggest that you will contact a substitute teacher if Cynthia would like to spend the rest of the day alone with you.

5. Have the secretary inform the hospital that you are returning with Cynthia, but only tell her you both are going for a ride.

6. Tell Cynthia that you were really worried about her because you are legally responsible for her welfare during school hours. Scold her for walking barefoot as this violates the school dress code, and dismiss the entire incident.

A SAUCY SCIENCE SESSION!

While you had not intended to teach in a big city school, you gladly agree to replace a teacher who has taken a leave of absence for the last three months of school. A three-day veteran, you are pleased with the response of your six- and seven-year-olds about "brainstorming" the signs of spring. James, your scribe, is writing the children's ideas on the blackboard—with a little assistance from you.

With his new responsibility and active involvement James seems to be responding nicely. Yesterday he really shook your confidence when, in the middle of a quiet activity period, he called you a "bitch." Because you couldn't dismiss class you scolded him and then talked with him privately after school. He apologized—without any prompting from you—so you talked with him, trying to win his allegiance, for the sociogram you gave the class, in an effort to determine its social dynamics, identifies James as a class leader. Your next step was to get him to act as your assistant at the blackboard.

You are brought back to the present by an unsynchronized chorus of voices reporting that James has written a naughty word on the blackboard. One quick glance reveals that the list now reads:

robins
thundershowers
warmer weather
pussy

You look at James who smirks while explaining that he is waiting for you to spell "willow." Some of the children are quizzing others about the word's meaning, and the rest are rolling in the aisles with laughter, watching to see how you will react.

Noises of bedlam reach the main office, from which your principal bolts to investigate the disturbance. As he appears in the doorway, you have a few decisions to make. All eyes are awaiting your next move.

YOUR SOLUTION

YOUR REACTIONS TO THE ALTERNATE SOLUTIONS

ALTERNATE SOLUTIONS

1. Spell "willow" for James in your most calm, but commanding voice, and casually invite the principal to join this exciting activity.

2. Have the class apologize to the principal for disturbing other classes with their noise, and hope that he leaves you alone to handle this situation yourself.

3. Instruct James to accompany the principal to his office. Tell the principal that James is "inciting a riot" and that you will privately explain the circumstances in detail to him later.

4. Ignore the principal's presence and invent some explanation that will satisfy everyone; then hurry on to the next sign of spring.

5. Ask one of the "rollers" to define the word and discuss why some words are not appropriate for school or children.

6. Jump into your Sex Education unit immediately while the motivation is optimal and the readiness factor exists.

MYSTERIOUS MARTY

Moving from your two-year position in a ghetto neighborhood school to a newly landscaped, freshly painted suburban school was the best morale booster you could have provided yourself this year. Your excitement with the modern facilities and abundance of equipment and materials soon dwindles, however, with the arrival of your sixth-graders.

Although well-dressed, your students confront you with anxiety and hostility. Your first responsibility, separating a fistfight, results in one boy, Marty, sprawled across the path of your principal and several parents visiting the school. You retrieve Marty, apoligize, and initiate a class discussion of what you expect in classroom behavior. Evidently the only consensus the class can reach is that you should be taught a few lessons. In unusual moments when they aren't concentrating on you, they are ruthlessly bullying each other. Bowie knives, razor blades, and nails confiscated from the shop area are among the arsenal you've collected in a few hours.

Several weeks later you are progressing in your effort to channel this energy and brain power into a relevant curriculum, and you have discovered why things are working pretty well: Marty isn't a key agitator anymore. Too preoccupied to notice sooner, you realize that whenever Marty attends class he sleeps. As you awaken him his buddy snarls, "He keeps a busy schedule nightly so he's got to sleep sometime!"

That night your problems are compounded. Driving home from a late-evening performance of the school orchestra, you nearly run over four boys darting across the street from a corner drug store—you are pretty sure one of the boys is Marty. Having pulled to the curb for a moment to gather your thoughts, your concern mounts when a police car appears and a screaming druggist points in the direction of the fleeing boys. Shaken and uncertain, you continue home to spend the rest of the night unsuccessfully attempting to confirm whether or not it was Marty.

What action are you prepared to take?

YOUR SOLUTION

YOUR REACTIONS TO THE ALTERNATE SOLUTIONS

ALTERNATE SOLUTIONS

1. Take a day of "sick leave" to give yourself more time to think through your responsibility in handling this situation.

2. Confide in your principal and seek his advice.

3. Visit Marty's home to discuss his poor attention and attendance and try to confirm his whereabouts last night. Allude to the possibility of police trouble if he continues his current attitudes and habits.

4. Invite Marty to dinner with your family so you can confront him with your suspicions in an environment more comfortable than school.

5. Stop speculating and anonymously inform the police of your suspicions so they can investigate Marty's innocence.

6. Visit the druggist to get a description of the boys to see if any could have been Marty.

KNOW-IT-ALL NANCY

There is usually one in every class, but you've never seen any nine-year-old to match Nancy's self-assurance and vocalization. Whenever you raise a question, ask for suggestions, or initiate a discussion, Nancy verbalizes her conclusions before you've completed your thought or her classmates have had an opportunity to think. Forcefully monopolizing the situation, she completes your sentences (if you take a breath), interprets the thoughts of others, and "puts down" her classmates, reminding all of her superiority. And she is superior—at least academically.

Your major concern is Nancy's insensitivity to the feelings of others as evidenced by her lack of positive relationships. Due to her egotistical air and constant verbal condemnations, her peers seldom voice their opinions and ideas openly. They have withdrawn, yet she seems unaware of their behavior. Tactful discussions, suggestions, and reprimands are obviously not helping Nancy.

The situation reaches new dimensions one day when Bobby, probably the most even-tempered boy in your class and one of Nancy's only friends, bellows, "Nancy, will you shut your mouth! You talk so much I can't even think and I intend to figure this one out for myself!" While you would like to agree with Bobby, that might not be the best way to break the sudden silence in the room.

Your move.

YOUR SOLUTION

YOUR REACTIONS TO THE ALTERNATE SOLUTIONS

ALTERNATE SOLUTIONS

1. Ask Nancy to verbalize how she feels about Bobby's outrage, and draw upon student participation to increase Nancy's social sensitivity.

2. Scold Bobby for his rudeness and demand an apology for Nancy.

3. Reserve any action until you observe what transpires without your interference.

4. Usher Nancy aside to privately discuss reasons for Bobby's reaction and ways she created her own problem.

5. Your response to Bobby: "Thank you! I was about to say the same thing in a kinder manner that might not have been as effective."

ESTABLISHING RAPPORT

Your happiness and success in teaching depend upon the effectiveness of your relationships with pupils. The heart of this relationship rests with how you perceive yourself and your pupils with respect to individual worth, needs, aspirations, operant value systems, and other influences. Studies have revealed that the psychologically healthy individual is characteristically an effective teacher. Teaching is indeed a human relations affair!

Your interactions with pupils will reflect your system of values and beliefs. Insistence that every first-year pupil learn to read by June, or that each pupil complete the same assignment at the same time is a value-based decision. Discussions in a faculty lounge reveal a potpourri of values and beliefs:

"Joan was delighted when she wrote her name perfectly for the first time!"

"Today's students fear nothing! How are we to punish them?"

"We were late for Art again . . . seems I just can't drag them away from their Science experiments!"

"Tom never has his mind on his work. I don't know what I'm going to do with him!"

Totally immersed in making value judgments and decisions, you will be teaching, consciously and unconsciously, attitudes and values through your behavior as well as the experiences you provide learners. There will be days of frustration when your behavior contradicts your beliefs, when a migraine headache eradicates your interest and ability to remain calm, patient, and understanding. The Socratic challenge "Know Thyself" is crucial to your success in developing quality relationships with children.

In any discussion of pupil-teacher interactions, motivation and discipline consistently monopolize attention. Motivation, though frequently discussed in extrinsic terms, is most powerful and enduring when it is intrinsic. Such motivation is observable when a learner is intently involved in an activity personally meaningful to him. Extrinsic motivation, however, is more prevalent in classrooms where teachers spend ten minutes trying to generate interest in an activity or threaten punishment when a paper is incomplete. This situation promotes the reversion to such concepts as discipline, class control, and behavior modification, instead of logical questions such as "Why am I teaching this?" and "Is this really relevant to the lives of these students at this time?"

Discipline has its intrinsic and extrinsic aspects also. Self-discipline is generally fostered when each pupil is treated with respect, when in your friendly, assured way, you preserve his self-concept by making reasonable requests, when you praise his accomplishments, and when you keep mutually established class rules to a minimum and clarify limitations. These elements encourage harmonious pupil-teacher relations. The extrinsic side of the discipline coin originates from two sources: peer pressure, which is most influential, and adult (teacher and parent) pressure. As you might expect, adult pressures prevail in formal education, or so we assume. You will soon discover vehement disagreements among teachers about the nature of good and bad behavior and how bad should be modified. The range of ideas concerns itself with a learner, his inherent nature, and such external standards as group norms or grade-level expectations. At one end of the continuum are teachers who feel any behavior OTHER than obedient, industrious, passive, attentive reaction is misconduct. Some, convinced that a deviation from law and order is a personal affront, are threatened and intimidated. A third set view misbehavior as symptomatic of deeper problems that they must identify to alleviate. Completing the gamut are teachers who believe that children should be given unqualified freedom to be themselves and do their own thing.

Somewhere within this range you will discover conditions in which you will operate comfortably and effectively. Your personal style will be determined by an interplay of your value system and physical/psychological tolerance. In any case, you will have to consider the causes of misconduct, usually attributed to boredom, frustration, failure, and a need for attention. It is essential that any correctional measures you undertake in striving for desirable behavior correlate with this goal.

Take, for instance, Dorothy's situation. She has been severely reprimanded for talking to her neighbor during a test. Her punishment is to stay after school to write "I will *never* talk during a test!" 100 times. What are the values she is learning? Will her activity and embarrassment change her needs or modify her future behavior? Will the change be desirable?

If the ultimate aim in education is self-disciplined, creative, and critical thinkers, you should be student oriented when exploring behavior—yours and theirs. Each person reacts differently to a system of rewards and punishments. A child physically punished at home may conclude that you don't like him when you ignore the same deviant behavior at school. Your relationship with a quiet child may be shattered if you are the first to scream condemnations (heaven forbid!) at him. In addition to knowing yourself, you must know the nature of each learner, his personality, social rapport, socioeconomic background, cultural beliefs, and history of academic success or failure. If creating healthy, open relationships with youngsters is a worthy goal, consideration must be given to these aspects of the child, and provisions for a system of differentiated discipline must be initiated in meeting the needs of each! Success plays a key role in daily human growth and development.

In grappling with your concepts of pupil-teacher interpersonal relationships, there are a few more points to ponder. Is learning or completing daily tasks the central issue of school for children? When a child maintains his independence, is he necessarily rebellious? When he guesses about an answer, is he to be condemned? If he inquires with perseverance, is he misbehaving? Is your role to generate convergence or divergence? Are your values in conflict with the learner's? Have you given any thought to the withdrawn child who is not the least bit disruptive? Are there some who like to think rather than talk? Is your concern with manipulating and controlling children rather than understanding them? What influence do you have in shaping a learner's perception about himself, and others? How significant is the misbehavior? How frequent?

Becoming a teacher is a never-ending, exhausting, and exhilarating process of testing and redefining personal values and beliefs about yourself, individual learners, and the learning process. Problems arise when this cycle is interrupted and on-the-spot decisions, irrespective of their ramifications, are made. Frequently such decisions are made because they make a teacher's life easier, more expedient, and/or safer. When this happens, a vital question surfaces: Do our classrooms exist for the convenience and security of teachers . . . or are they to provide pupils, who are learning to love, with a love of learning?

FOR FURTHER READING

ASCD. *Perceiving, Behaving, Becoming: A New Focus on Education.* Washington, D.C.: Association for Supervision and Curriculum Development, NEA, 1962.

ASCD. *To Nurture Humaneness.* Washington, D.C.: Association for Supervision and Curriculum Development, NEA, 1970.

Clarizio, Harvey F. *Toward Positive Classroom Discipline.* New York: John Wiley and Sons, 1971.

Combs, Arthur W., and Donald Syngg. *Individual Behavior.* New York: Harper & Row, 1959.

Gnagey, William J. *The Psychology of Discipline in the Classroom.* New York: The Macmillan Co. 1968.

Herndon, James. *The Way its Spozed To Be.* New York: Simon and Schuster, 1968.

Johnson, Kenneth R. *Teaching the Culturally Disadvantaged: A Rational Approach.* Chaps. 1-5. Palo Alto: Science Research Associates, 1970.

Kelley, Earl C. *Humanizing the Education of Children: A Philosophical Statement.* Washington, D.C.: American Association of Elementary-Kindergarten-Nursery Educators, NEA, 1969.

Kohl, Herbert. *36 Children.* New York: The New American Library, 1967.

Marshall, Catherine. *Christy.* New York: Avon Books, 1967.

Russell, Ivan L. *Motivation.* Dubuque: William C. Brown Co., 1971.

CHAPTER TWO

Learning Center Climate

CLASSROOM NUISANCES

The pleasures of your student-teaching experiences, which you took for granted, are now in proper perspective. Then you were able to work with individuals at a relaxed pace while days went by smoothly. What you wouldn't do for sharing some of your responsibility today, at the conclusion of your first week in the classroom.

The educational bureaucracy introduced in your week of orientation was palatable compared to the irritants and nuisances of your daily life in the classroom! This morning, for instance, five children sharpened pencils, and sharpened pencils, and sharpened pencils; one child came in late so his attendance card had to be retrieved from the office; Bobby, bending over to pick up a book, struck his head on his desk, emptying the contents on the floor, and came up with a huge lump that required a nurse's observation, which in turn required a hall pass and a volunteer to assist Bobby. A couple of potential aeronautical engineers sent paper piper cubs soaring around your ear as you wrote on the blackboard, and the frequently used john door developed a loud squeak. A water fight erupted at the sink, and every other minute someone else was asking, "What shall I do next?" when he finished in ten minutes the task that took you forty minutes to prepare.

It seems as though you're spending more time getting underway than you are teaching, and you can't tolerate a whole year of this. With the weekend coming up, explore solutions for your problems.

YOUR SOLUTION

YOUR REACTIONS TO THE ALTERNATE SOLUTIONS

ALTERNATE SOLUTIONS

1. Provide a supply of extra paper, pencils, erasers, and so forth that students can borrow at any time.

2. Establish a specific time during the day when children go to their lockers, sharpen pencils, and use the lavatory.

3. Develop a list of "things to do in your free time" with your pupils daily.

4. Develop a file of independent activities from which a pupil can choose a project to complete by himself or with friends.

5. Have the pupils identify classroom problems, propose solutions, and vote on which solutions they want to use.

"WHAT MAKES FRIDAY SPECIAL?"

Monday

Dear Mrs. Formal,

You're the best teacher we've ever had and the smartest. That's why we know you'll be able to tell us the answer to a confusing issue that has bugged us since the first week of school. What makes Friday special? Why is it the only day we have a free reading period instead of reading groups? Another thing, why can't we have a "scramble" day every day? We *like* doing our work if we can choose its order and how long we'll spend on each subject. Could we spread fun activities like science experiments, dramatic productions, and art projects evenly throughout the week? And about playground activities—the last two Fridays it's been a downpour out there so couldn't we just go out when the weather is good and you think we need a break? Monday-Thursday it's dullsville with everyone really waiting for Friday when we are allowed to do our own thing—more or less. We could get our independent projects done better if we didn't have a week in between each time we worked on them. Couldn't we do creative writing better if we did it when we feel groovy? Can't we relax, have fun, and learn Monday through Friday? Besides, we like you better on Friday.

Your 6th graders
R.S.V.P.

Finding this note on your desk blotter, what are you going to do?

YOUR SOLUTION

YOUR REACTIONS TO THE ALTERNATE SOLUTIONS

ALTERNATE SOLUTIONS

1. Pretend you never got it!
2. Explain your reasoning to the class.
3. Give them more opportunities to make individual choices and decisions about their daily activities.
4. Survey your planbook and schedule at least one activity you know they like each day.

"YOU'RE BEING PAID TO TEACH US . . ."

"Power to the people" is the current motto of your fifth graders, but you've been slow to realize they don't want it themselves—or so they claim. Given a choice about anything, they wait for you to clue them in to a direction. When involved in inductive learnings or value clarification, some argue, "You're being paid to teach us so why don't you do it?" One says, "Tell me the answers and I'll listen." Another demands, "Give me a test and I'll show you what I've learned."

Your discussions about learning to think for themselves seem to have fallen on deaf ears. Any ideas on how to change this attitude?

YOUR SOLUTION

YOUR REACTIONS TO THE ALTERNATE SOLUTIONS

ALTERNATE SOLUTIONS

1. Prepare a lecture describing the benefits of learning to think for oneself and emphasizing that the students' role is not to please a teacher but to learn how to learn.

2. Project the status of your students' future following their requests of you and yours of them; then have a couple of children role play these predictions and decide which kind of situation they'd prefer.

3. View a film of a classroom that depicts the kind of teacher they are requesting and discuss how they would feel and what they would learn under these circumstances.

4. Consider these criticisms as typical reactions in transferring from teacher-directed to student-directed learning, and make no revisions in your plans, hoping the students' attitudes will change with their experiences of adjustment.

THE DILEMMA OF INTEREST CENTERS

"Mom made this for us!"

"Dad and I assembled this!"

The many proud comments of your jubilant fifth graders resound as they make inquisitive rounds among the new interest centers. This was one of your solutions to challenging the wide range of abilities, interests, and needs of your supposedly homogeneously grouped class, but without your parent volunteers the centers would never have been ready to operate today. In addition to making materials, audio tape recordings, and study guides for visuals you outlined, they adapted successful home activities for classroom use. They claim not only to have enjoyed it but also to have learned a lot!

As your day begins you point out the attractive signs—Math, Science, Art, Games, Language Arts, Social Studies—and elaborate on the conditions and procedures for using these centers: cooperation, consideration for working neighbors, orderly replacement of materials, and a maximum of four at a center.

Proceeding with a business-as-usual attitude becomes difficult, to say the least, when you realize all thoughts are on the center activities. By lunchtime, you're convinced the whole idea was the product of insanity! There are disputes over possession of products; materials have been abused and left in disorder; some children quickly complete their required tasks, others do not, yet all proceed to centers anyway; and the noise level in the room has increased beyond a safe decibel range!

While unwinding in the faculty lounge during lunch, other less obvious perceptions bother you. The shy children who desperately need social interaction didn't participate, nor did some of those who most need to work with manipulatives. Some children couldn't make a choice where to become involved, so they roamed. Others may never use more than one center unless somehow they're encouraged to broaden their interests.

How can you get the students to cooperate effectively in using these centers, and in such a way that you can work simultaneously with groups of children?

YOUR SOLUTION

YOUR REACTIONS TO THE ALTERNATE SOLUTIONS

ALTERNATE SOLUTIONS

1. Design a daily schedule that provides each child with an opportunity to use at least one center.

2. Limit the use of centers to cooperative, mature, independent students you can trust.

3. Assign a monitor to check whether a student has his work completed before he can proceed to the centers.

4. Explain operational procedures and why they are necessary for effective use of the centers.

5. Use the centers as a substitute for daily seat work and an integral part of curriculum and instruction, rather than a reward for finishing work and an experience above and beyond instructional requirements.

PRIDE AND PREJUDICE

Your physician attributed your indigestion to a nervous stomach, but you insist that the general attitude of your class is the major contributor. These multi-age intermediate students consistently create disagreeable situations whenever they interact, which is all of the time.

Not only are they poor losers but they are also ungracious winners. Indoor and outdoor activities, whether sport, game, or academic exercise, digress into individual battles. The victors of a softball game brag about beating the "pansies" of the other team; the losers call foul play and give excuses for their loss, often at the expense of individual players. Teamed in pairs to solve a math problem, they argue over who first arrived at the solution if it is right, and they accuse each other for the error when it is wrong.

More aggravating than their competitiveness is their evident concept of normalcy. Anyone who behaves, believes, or owns something different from the others is weird, queer, and abnormal. Kevin brought a new game to share with the class that he had received for Hanukkah. As a consequence the game was ignored and Kevin was chided about Jewish holidays and customs. James, who couldn't attend the Valentine's Day party because his religious beliefs would be violated, was the subject of ridicule that culminated in a fistfight. Sue and Sunny, Chinese twins, are frequently harangued because of their slanted eyes.

Where will you begin to improve this situation?

YOUR SOLUTION

YOUR REACTIONS TO THE ALTERNATE SOLUTIONS

ALTERNATE SOLUTIONS

1. Provide a reward for even the smallest incidence of kind, cooperative behavior.

2. Allow children who can peacefully work together to do so; all others will be omitted from team learning until they exhibit a tolerance for differences among their classmates.

3. Dividing your class into halves, title one sector "the good guys" and the other "the bad guys." The former will discriminate against and harass the latter until noon, when their roles are switched. Near the end of the afternoon discuss each of the roles and their accompanying feelings and behaviors.

4. In a group setting, problem solve your situation through an illustration. For instance, how would the children feel and what problems would be created if: All toys were identical? The sky was always overcast? Clothes were only made of blue wool? Everyone were seven feet tall? Relate this discussion to your own problems.

FACILITATING A CLIMATE
FOR LEARNING

Feelings and attitudes are central issues in establishing a learning climate—a proper atmosphere and environment. Earl Kelley suggests, "How a person feels about what he knows is more important than what he knows." Your combined beliefs about learning and the process through which each pupil is to achieve his maximum capacity as a productive, happy member of society will shape each child's attitudes: attitudes about himself as a person and learner, about school, about yourself and teachers in general, about subject matter, about adults and society. The climate you initiate will provide guidelines for your pupils' physical, psychological, social, and intellectual behavior. Charles Silberman has accused teachers of making decisions in a state of "mindlessness." Hopefully, having studied the cases and reflected on these problems, you will be among the exceptions to this statement. Learning climate is one aspect of teaching that is often taken for granted or ignored.

Learning instigated by intrinsic motivation is far more profitable than that of extrinsic. If not used as a focal point, pupil interests must at least be a major influence in curricular decisions. Success motivates learning. Building a backlog of success provides a tolerance for failure, as the chief motive of human behavior is a need for self-esteem and a feeling of personal adequacy. Readiness is an inherent factor in success. Persistence in teaching a child before he is ready to learn is a waste of teacher time, and in addition the child develops attitudes of avoidance that may interfere with later learning. Nevertheless, student's readiness to learn can be developed.

Because cooperation is a necessary element in society, it seems only natural to provide a variety of learning experiences in which success can be obtained only through cooperative efforts. A sense of social responsibility can be acquired whether a pupil is alternately teacher, learner, leader, or follower. This group inquiry process is an overlooked or incidental aspect of learning for which opportunities should be deliberately planned. A second aspect of learning deals with personal inquiry, providing a learner with the time, space, and materials to pursue his interests privately or with a friend. This frequent occurrence should have your full support and encouragement. Differentiated and individualized study is the final major provision for you to consider. It will be an enormous task to diagnose pupil needs and interests and provide each with a tailor-made instructional program appropriate to his attitudes, needs, and interests.

True, a teacher cannot provide thirty pupils with all of these opportunities daily, nor do you have to! In fact, some of your goals would be defeated were you to establish yourself as the sole learning resource. Pupils learn from experiences and their consequences. They learn a great deal from one another. This is one of the most incredible, until close examination, revelations an adult perceives in a learning situation. One child, in teaching a skill or concept to another, communicates it more quickly and easily than you might while reinforcing his own thinking about it. As the learner's eyes light up, you will say to yourself, "Why didn't I think of that?" The longer your pupils are together, the more rapidly they will learn from each other. Among the many harvests you reap through your encouragement of this learning resource will be insights about your pupils, such as avenues of concept formation, communication patterns, and feelings.

Audio-visual materials are more than mere learning aids. As a learning resource they reinforce and expand a learner's world, increasing his perceptions, stimulating new thoughts and generating new concepts. Considering the visual emphasis of this and future generations, formal education must begin to include the study and use of commercial, as well as those distinguished as educational, media. Independently or collectively, televised programs, audio and video records, single-concept film loops, filmstrips, films, commercial and instructional records, slides, and view masters are all paramount sources of learning. Each presents viewing and/or listening opportunities a student should learn to employ for his own purposes. He must be taught to assimilate such information through a critical eye. Throughout this process he may apply, incorporate, and increase his learnings by developing his own media of expression through such vehicles as photography, sculpture, and drawing.

A good sense of humor and the resources explored above can bring "life" to the learning climate, which too often has been a lonely, dull, and unrewarding place for children and teachers. Now both can become involved in satisfying social and intellectual exchanges. The learner's opportunities must be relevant from his point of view and significant to his growth. The atmosphere must be one in which he is allowed to inquire, hypothesize, experiment, evaluate, and so on. There should be freedom to react emotionally as well as academically, to discuss problems openly, and to move responsibly in the learning environment. Quiet and active periods might be spontaneously determined by learner and teacher needs. It might be important to note that mild emotion usually enhances learning.

As the world of educators continues to argue the inexhaustible question of how to group pupils to provide the most effective learning potential, the question of learning should be foremost. Attempts to achieve group homogeneity customarily rely on a solitary criterion such as reading achievement, thus ignoring obvious group diversities such as social maturity, interests, and academic potential. Frequently students are tracked based upon this one criterion, regardless of their aptitude and ability in other areas. Essentially, any graded school organization only assures that pupils in a class will be approximately the same age. Can this be a crucial criterion in effective learning?

Heterogeneity is a teaching asset! Within a heterogeneous class, you can group and regroup into friendship, interest, achievement, and ability groups depending upon your objectives, thus capitalizing on the diversity. Each learner gleans perceptions about himself and others as he travels throughout his "mini-world," while beginning to learn, with guidance, the meaning of cooperation, competition, tolerance, and individuality, among others. His learning center is enriched by a variety of temperaments, abilities, achievements, strengths and weaknesses. It is within this realm that his growth and development as an individual must be nurtured.

When learning is student centered, active student participation in problem solving and decision making flourishes, for when students select and plan an activity, they eagerly engage in it. So, too, do they enjoy the responsibility of establishing regulations for their working conditions and maintaining the upkeep of their environment. Their feeling of "belongingness" increases with their participation, and it reinforces their awareness of group expectations.

Facilitating this atmosphere should be the goal in selecting equipment and materials. They should be stimulating, manipulative and interactive, attractive, and meaningful to the learners. Encompassing multilevels of skill and concept development or reinforcement, presentations must be varied to suit differing learning styles.

Interest centers can be implemented to assist learning. They may include pupil resources such as collections and hobbies, audio-visual media, and interactive media such as games and simulations. They might be curriculum oriented, such as Art, Science and Math, or in the case of some topics, Creativity, for instance, they may be interdisciplinary in nature. Uses of these centers may range from pure relaxation to topic introduction, to application for skills previously acquired. A Reading Center might be carpeted and scattered with pillows, hidden with room dividers, and overflowing with pupil-selected library books, child and adult periodicals, and the daily newspaper. A center such as this invites private and cooperative explorations. The children love to contribute to and learn from these centers.

There are many ways to approach learning! You will have to rely upon your resourcefulness and that of your pupils. While time and money are important to building a rich storehouse of learning experiences, you will be amazed at what your combined efforts will produce.

The real imperative in achieving a climate for learning is summarized in the proverb that follows:

I hear, and I forget,
I see, and I remember,
I do, and I understand.

FOR FURTHER READING

ASCD. *Life Skills in School and Society.* Washington, D.C.: Association for Supervision and Curriculum Development, NEA, 1969.

Leonard, George B. *Education and Ecstasy.* New York: Dell Publishing Co., 1968.

Holt, John. *How Children Learn.* New York: Pitman, 1967.

Kelley, Earl C. *Education for What is Real.* New York: Harper, 1947.

LaBenne, Wallace D. *Educational Implications of Self-Concept Theory.* Pacific Palisades, Calif.: Goodyear Publishing Co., 1969.

Mager, Robert F. *Developing Attitude Toward Learning.* Palo Alto: Fearon Publishers, 1968.

Rogers, Carl R. *Freedom to Learn.* Columbus: Charles E. Merrill Publishing Co., 1969.

Silberman, Charles E. *Crisis in the Classroom: The Remaking of American Education.* New York: Random House, 1970.

Torrance, E. Paul, and R. E. Myers. *Creative Learning and Teaching.* New York: Dodd, Mead and Co., 1970.

CHAPTER THREE

Personalized Education

SNOWBALL'S HAPPENING

A first-year teacher, you never fully realized how the principles of individualizing applied to whole group experience until "Snowball." Snowball is a white lab rat you borrowed from a doctor friend as a new classroom addition. While briefing you about her care and handling, the doctor reveals that Snowball is pregnant.

As the days go on and Snowball's physique alters, the eight-, nine-, and ten-year-olds who are as yet unaware of her condition begin to speculate about tumors, obesity, and pregnancy. Inquisitively noting dramatic changes in her housekeeping habits, they become very concerned and considerate as her due date approaches. Although they haven't been told, they are certain she is pregnant and from their experience exchange the very best explanations about birth and baby care. A small group of children spend time in the library investigating animal births and report, with remarkable ease and accuracy, their findings to their classmates.

The big day finally arrives.

"Why is Snowball sitting like that?"
"Look! Something's in the cage . . . and it's alive."
"That's her baby . . ."
"Now there are twins, triplets . . .WOW! What do you call four babies? Quad what?"

"A dozen pups—she must have taken fertility pills!"
"Why are they bald? My father told me age and worry make people bald!"
"Ye gads! Seventeen!!!! She'll have a heart attack from overexertion."
"You knew that she was pregnant all along! Why didn't you tell us? Why didn't she quit after six or seven?"
"How is she going to be able to be in seventeen places all at once?"
"What are birth control pills?"
"Where are they eyes? Can they hear us now?"
"Snowball looks tired!"

How are you going to satisfy these inquiries without boring the children who have already lost interest in Snowball or offending parents who are against any kind of sex education in school?

YOUR SOLUTION

YOUR REACTIONS TO THE ALTERNATE SOLUTIONS

ALTERNATE SOLUTIONS

1. Ignore the questions you feel you shouldn't answer.

2. Arrange an interview with your doctor friend for the youngsters who are interested in pursuing the issues.

3. Request a panel of parents to act as resources for the children.

4. Rely upon the students who investigated animal births to supply the answers.

5. Begin your sex education unit now that the pupils have a common foundation of experience in which to relate new knowledge, and don't worry about parent reactions.

READING IS FOR THE BIRDS!

Mary is waiting for the other ten to finish; Jane, Mary's shadow, i
through as soon as Mary, yet you know she didn't read the selection with
any comprehension; Robert and Thomas fidget uncomfortably while stil
on the second page. Occasionally the others ask what this or that word i
and then read on. Twenty minutes pass before the last child finishes, so
you have ten minutes to discuss what was read; you'd like to spend mor
time, but you have three more groups—the Bluebirds, Cardinals, Humming
birds—to see this morning.

As the Sparrows leave for their other activities, you reflect on the man
obvious problems of your reading program: the new vocabulary is old fo
some; the effective readers read the story two months ago, while th
poorer readers in the same group need concentrated skill development; th
rest of the class not only realizes but emphasizes that the Sparrows ar
"dumb and dull," which carries over into peer relationships; you ar
wasting fifteen to twenty minutes per group sitting while the children read
silently; the faster readers are as bored as you are and gaze out the window
to freedom.

The oral reading aspect on Thursdays also makes a poor program i
your eyes. The Hummingbirds, with petrified eyes, stumble along th
unfriendly printed line, presenting a weak model of oral fluency; th
Bluebirds see no reason to reread orally a story they read silently; th
Cardinals keep plodding along; and the Sparrows seem to be goin
nowhere.

No one is building a love for reading. How will you alleviate th
situation?

YOUR SOLUTION

YOUR REACTIONS TO THE ALTERNATE SOLUTIONS

ALTERNATE SOLUTIONS

1. Continue the organization but set aside one day a week for "free reading."

2. Establish an Independent Reading Program using library books to be selected by the pupils and read at their own rate.

3. Establish skill groups, of fluctuating membership, and pupil team your class for all other reading activities.

4. Develop job sheets and study guides for each story, hold conferences with pupils, and let them work at their own rate in the social organization they choose.

5. Plan with your students for an improved approach to reading.

SIGNIFICANT STANLEY

A warm glow fills you when you think of Stanley! This gifted eight-year-old's IQ leaps off the testing scales, his baby fat remains on his small frame, and his insatiable curiosity coupled with an impish grin are fascinating; he constantly amazes you. Academically talented, socially well-adjusted, and physically uncoordinated, Stanley waddles ducklike down the corridor, poking his head into classrooms saying, "Good morning" or "Have a good night!" to teachers and joking with his peers. He is known by the entire school population for his gregarious wit, happiness, and brains.

His reading program includes a linguistic series so new that the commercial answer keys for the materials aren't available. Frequently you will find him by your side requesting "a conference." He will then review the items he's marked as questionable and provide logical reasoning for having more than one "right" answer. As he thinks through the exercises with you, you discover he is accurate 99 percent of the time and accepts your explanations on the other occasions. "Thank goodness you don't have an answer key!" he says as he returns to his tasks. He really loves the challenge of substantiating his conclusions and thoroughly enjoys your reactions.

One day in the faculty lounge your principal inquires about Stanley's progress and asks for your professional opinion about whether Stan is correctly placed in your continuous progress, multi-aged primary class. You know that his parents are emphatic about keeping Stan with his social peers as long as possible, for they feel that this is as important to Stanley's growth as his academic progress. They believe that with the right teacher at school and plenty of stimulation at home, Stanley will encounter challenging experiences. How will you respond to your principal?

YOUR SOLUTION

YOUR REACTIONS TO THE ALTERNATE SOLUTIONS

ALTERNATE SOLUTIONS

1. Relate that Stanley's attitude toward learning, relationships with his peers, and interactions with you are pretty convincing evidence that he is accurately placed.

2. Recommend that he should be in a class for the gifted.

3. Suggest that because of his social maturity he should be placed with intermediate children.

4. Convey the essentials of Stanley's continuous progress program to allow your principal to draw his own conclusions.

TECHNOLOGY HUMANIZES?

"Let each become all he is capable of being," your college's motto, is exactly what you are trying to do as a beginning teacher. Daily you encourage positive attitudes in interpersonal relations, wholesome attitudes toward differences, and keen interest in personal learning and discovery. You find all of this very difficult with twenty-nine children until you discover the value of electronics and technology! Such things as commercial TV programming offer a perfect opportunity to study social sciences and human emotion. This is just one instance of many in which media serve as a dynamic teaching device, initiating student involvement that allows you to assume so much more latitude in your guidance and administrative roles as well as in individualized instruction.

Yet you are beginning to feel that at least some of your colleagues are misconstruing your intentions. An indication of this problem is revealed in the Art teacher's comment, "Don't you dare leave this room until your 'mechanical zoo' is disconnected and your children are back in their seats!" Later that day in the faculty lounge you are greeted with, "There's the one who is all caught up in our materialistic society of gadgets, gimmicks, knobs, and cords!" Another adds, "I thought you liked working with children but its apparent that you'd rather have them working with machines." A third concludes, "If you impinge on my curriculum areas, next year when I have your children I'll send them back to you and you can keep them busy!"

What is your response to their thoughts?

YOUR SOLUTION

YOUR REACTIONS TO THE ALTERNATE SOLUTIONS

ALTERNATE SOLUTIONS

1. Invite the other teachers into your "mechanical zoo" for a first-hand analysis of your organization and resources used by learners, as well as to see how often you teach small groups of children.

2. Spend your only free period this day explaining your rationale for incorporating machines as instructional resources.

3. Side-step their opinions and initiate a new topic of conversation.

4. Challenge them to give suggestions about more effective ways to individualize instruction for all the students and to provide frameworks for learning.

PURCHASE POWER

Moving into the room of a 25-year career teacher, who must have been a pack rat, isn't easy! Every spare minute the first six weeks of school you spend clearing out his materials and reorganizing supplies; then you move in your teaching materials. The already irritating situation becomes deplorable when you learn budget requests for next year are due in three weeks. You've been so busy "housecleaning" that you don't even know what resources are available in your school!

Your requisition form has two columns; supplies and materials. An educated guess from the size of your supply inventory suggests that the same order was submitted for 25 consecutive years! You are convinced you could furnish the entire district's requisition for ruled, construction, crepe, and toilet paper and still have some left over. Your quantity of chalk and pencils laid end to end would, without a doubt, reach to the moon! Stacked boxes of paper clips, fasteners, staples, and rulers completely fill a 6' x 3' shelf. It appears that it would be wise to spend the supplies allocation for some much needed materials.

Unfortunately, you discover that the monies allocated for supplies and materials come from different budgets so you can't spend your supply money on materials. However, your principal decides to compensate your materials sum from another budget and you go home loaded down with literature on the latest educational materials.

Wall-to-wall catalogues and brochures surround you as you begin your shopping spree. The further you shop, the more confused you become. You discover that the educational market is flooded with new books, programmed materials, kits, packages, audio-visual aids incorporating any combination of kinesthetic, auditory, and/or visual approaches, etc. All purport to fulfill the same learning needs. Another discovery is that your once impressive-sounding expense account is quite limited in light of the costs of these materials.

What and how do you choose? How do you determine a system of priority? The decision is yours!

YOUR SOLUTION

YOUR REACTIONS TO THE ALTERNATE SOLUTIONS

ALTERNATE SOLUTIONS

1. Inventory the classroom equipment and materials you have and supplement them with multi-level ones you think essential for your curricular program.

2. Order absolute must items, but request that the remainder of your budget be held in abeyance until you know the personalized needs of next year's students.

3. Create a committee of students to make purchase recommendations and to give opinions on your selections.

4. To avoid duplication of expensive items, get together with a few colleagues when ordering and plan to share.

5. Invest in games and independent activities students can use to reinforce learnings and acquire other skills.

6. Purchase only those items that can easily be adapted to a wide range of objectives, interests, and settings.

INDIVIDUALIZING INSTRUCTION

Individualized or personalized instruction is a philosophical ideal that deserves your personal investigation and commitment. Definitions of individualized instruction generally refer to its nature and the degree to which it is implemented. Since it is student-oriented, the characteristics of each student influence the selection of his objectives, instruction, pace, and materials. His instruction may take the form of independent study or, at times when his learning needs, style, and rate approximate those of other learners, he may participate in team, small, or large group inquiry.

Far from a new concept, individualized instruction has been provided to some degree for exceptional children—usually considered the "slow" or "gifted"—while the majority of pupils study the same curricular unit in the same way over the same period of time. So, to some extent, individual differences have been recognized. Unfortunately, in most instances, the lip service extended to individualized instruction is seldom interpreted into teaching practices. It really can be achieved in practice!

Individualized instruction does not pertain to any special arrangement of student or teacher personnel, nor does it depend upon environmental conditions such as flexible scheduling or physical openness in a school plant. It can be implemented in horizontal (i.e. ability or interest groups) and vertical (i.e. lock-step, multi-age, nongraded) organizations. However, it does require rethinking the roles of teacher, student, instruction, and curriculum. Also, it necessitates a patient, imaginative teacher who, willing to begin in small steps, initiates differentiated instruction to meet at least some of the pupil differences.

John Holt contends children fail because we teach them. In an individualized setting, a teacher can no longer simply dispense knowledge or assume responsibility for teaching everything to each learner. A dangerous equation has been made between teaching and learning that is dispelled by today's teacher who realizes that much of a pupil's learning potential is lost when someone other than the child assumes the responsibility for his learning.

The teacher's new role is one of facilitation of learning, which includes three major functions: specialist, executive, and professional. Predominantly he is a specialist in human growth and development and the learning process as he diagnoses, prescribes, and measures the progress of each learner in a humanistic environment. As an executive, he coordinates human and material resources and organizes appropriate learning experiences. As a professional, he assumes the dual role of curriculum developer and innovator. Concerned with affective, psychomotor, and cognitive objectives, he needs a solid grasp of learning principles, concept development, and questioning skills in relation to the corresponding levels of thought each kind of question provokes.

Beginning with what the child feels and knows, the teacher prepares an appropriate learning program for him. In individualization, measurement of pupil progress is concerned with the child's advancement and achievements with respect to his potential and point of initial study, and not in comparison to some imaginary yardstick of perfection found in grade-level expectations.

In this stage a learner's role differs radically from what most of us experienced in formal education. He has a voice in fashioning learning experiences that will shape his individuality. Frequently, his experiences are self-selected, self-directed, self-paced, self-corrected, and self-appraised, with guidance—when he seeks it—from you, his learning consultant. His goal is independence, a basic human drive, in learning. He learns to question and takes great pride in his conquests. Cognizant of his own program, his habits result from his successes rather than repetitious activity. His concepts are integrated and crystalized through real-life applications. With a curriculum of no ceilings or boundaries, he employs an extensive amount of learning methods and resources.

Job sheets, study guides, programmed materials, and self-directing/ self-correcting materials used in conjunction with a variety of concrete or simulated models assist his learning. A learning packet on a single concept, for instance, might include:

1. A clear, simple statement of the concept;
2. Referent(s) physically accessible or adequately portrayed;
3. Behavioral objectives;
4. Proposed procedures and options;
5. Record sheets to indicate progress and note any questions and problems;
6. Self-administered/self-corrected test as a guide for review;
7. Some form of feedback for the teacher—from a written report to preparations to be made for a pupil-teacher conference.

More recently computers have been introduced as instructional resources. While a teacher may use them to assist in learning diagnosis and program planning, among other functions, a pupil may retrieve learning materials or perform intricate, mechanical tasks. The multiple uses and potential of this resource have yet to be completely explored.

To avoid risk of misinterpretation, further clarification may be advisable. The suggestions above as learning resources in no way indicate that the teacher is not needed or that his role ends when he has individuals and groups working at their level on relevant materials. There will be no time for a cup of coffee in the lounge. These resources allow him to see children and work with them when he is needed, as well as to present new concepts and skills at appropriate times in a child's progress. Believe me, you will have no time to unclutter the top of your desk until your pupils leave, and by then you may be too tired to care.

In preparing differentiated, and eventually individualized instruction, you will have to make decisions about learners and their learning climate, as reviewed in Chapters 1 and 2. Operationally, the biggest problem you will encounter is classroom management—planning, scheduling, and locating space for simultaneous group and independent activities. Your plans and schedule, of necessity, must be fluid and variable. It will take awhile for you and your students to feel comfortable in your new roles. Perhaps strategies and devices such as sociograms, sociodramas, role playing, and bibliotherapy will assist in smoother transitions.

When you begin to humanize the classroom through individualized instruction, you will discover elation as you perceive pupil potential unleashed. Gone are the days of planbooks used annually without change, and teachers worrying about being on page 147 by Thanksgiving. I hope!

FOR FURTHER READING

ASCD *Individualizing Instruction*. Washington, D.C.: Association for Supervision and Curriculum Development, NEA, 1964.

Goodlad, John I., and Robert H. Anderson *The Nongraded Elementary School*. New York: Harcourt, Brace & World, 1963.

Hillson, Maurie, and Joseph Bongo. *Continuous Progress Education: A Practical Approach*. Palo Alto: Science Research Associates, 1971.

Lee, Dorris M. *Diagnostic Teaching*. Washington, D.C.: American Association of Elementary-Kindergarten-Nursery Educators, NEA, 1970.

Mager, Robert F. *Preparing Instructional Objectives*. Palo Alto: Fearon Publishers, 1962.

Stahl, Dona Kofod, and Patricia Murphy Anzalone *Individualized Teaching in Elementary Schools*. West Nyack, N.J.: Parker Publishing Co., 1970.

Weinstein, Gerald, and Mario D. Fantini, eds. *Towards Humanistic Education: A Curriculum of Effect*. New York: Praeger Publishers, 1970.

Wolfson, Bernice J. *Moving Toward Personalized Learning and Teaching*. Encino, Calif.: International Center for Educational Development, 1969.

Woodruff, Asahel D. *Basic Concepts of Teaching*. San Francisco: Chandler Publishing Co., 1961.

CHAPTER FOUR

Measurement Considerations

NO ROOM FOR CREATIVITY

Working through the introduction to your initial creative writing lesson with your fourth graders, you are astounded by their ability to form ideas and express them creatively. Caught up in their contagious enthusiasm, you are delighted with their verbal involvement and so move on in your lesson to have each child try his hand at writing something creative. Your bubble bursts!

MERCEDES: Can we print or do we have to write?

YOU: Whatever you are most comfortable doing.

JANET: I don't know how to spell "motorcycle"!

YOU: Spell it the way it sounds . . . or maybe your neighbor knows how to spell it.

RONALD: I'm not going to do it! I'll get an "F" if I do and an "F" if I don't, so I choose not to waste my time!

YOU: We are dreaming up ideas and expressing them. Don't let worries about spelling and punctuation stop you! These papers won't be graded.

RONALD: Maybe you won't put a grade at the top but my paper will have more red ink on it than my pencil scribblings!

YOU: I have never done that and won't!

MICKEY: There's always a first time. Every other teacher does it so you will, too. They will teach you how!

JANE: I don't know whether to use a period or semicolon here.

MELODY: I can't find my eraser!!!

YOU: That's all right . . . just cross out your mistakes and go on.

MELODY: (sobbing quietly) If I do that then I'll spend all night with my mother looking over my shoulder while I rewrite this to show you that I can do neat work.

RONALD: Mary's done with hers! Since she always gets good marks, can I dictate my story to her while she writes it?

TED: I want to tell my story to the tape recorder so you won't be tempted to mark up my paper. Besides, then I won't be given the third degree by my mother since I'll have no paper to take home!

YOU: EVERYONE STOP IMMEDIATELY!

Your move.

YOUR SOLUTION

YOUR REACTIONS TO THE ALTERNATE SOLUTIONS

ALTERNATE SOLUTIONS

1. Pair your pupils into heterogeneous teams of one creative thinker and one confident writer and have them compose their thoughts together.

2. Divide your pupils into four or five groups to create composite stories.

3. Rather than reinforcing their negative attitudes, have volunteers read aloud their compositions and then give them the option of passing them in to you or keeping them.

4. Give your children a choice between keeping their creations private or sharing them with a friend.

5. Have the pupils exchange papers and help each other correct errors caught in proofreading, then collect their papers and make only positive comments on their ideas.

IS THIS ACCOUNTABILITY?

In a newly constructed open-climate school, you have the position of associate teacher teamed with two others and a team leader. Responsible for providing continuous progress programs in Language Arts and Social Sciences, you will be working with a multi-age group of nine- to twelve-year-olds. There are 120 students in your quad.

It takes but a few weeks for you to realize that, at least in your quad, the concept of open climate is limited exclusively to the architectural design of the school. The others in your team scorn the student freedoms and teaching approaches you establish, and they exhibit little respect for individual differences. You acquire immunity to their nonverbal disapproval as you persist in your efforts to give learning relevance on individual levels, but your evenings are spent wondering, "Why am I teaching this? Are there better methods I could be using? Can I see growth in any students as a result of my efforts? Can the students see their own progress?"

Near the end of the first reporting period, you prepare for a team meeting in which a consensus will be reached about the potential and progress of each student. This comprehensive statement will be recorded in permanent school files and mailed home to parents who will attend parent conferences.

At the team meeting the other three teachers open their grade books with test scores and discipline entries as you begin to shuffle the individual sheets you've developed on each learner. Your colleagues continually discuss individual comparisons in pupil achievement in terms of group norms regardless of your injections about individual growth since the beginning of school.

Completing the first of many reports, you conclude that the team consensus about each student will be determined by grades evenly distributed on a bell curve and incidents of disciplinary action. Nothing else is relevant to this group of teachers. What, if any, action will you take?

YOUR SOLUTION

YOUR REACTIONS TO THE ALTERNATE SOLUTIONS

ALTERNATE SOLUTIONS

1. Write a progress report addendum, including affective considerations and specific issues about each child you believe your colleagues are overlooking, and attach it to each student's record.

2. Take no action, for your colleagues have seniority in the team and must know what they are doing.

3. Interrupt the meeting with a speech about the goals of education and theories of learning your colleagues are dismissing in achieving their consensus.

4. Call parents to convey the information you believe is pertinent to student progress.

5. Meet with your principal and curriculum coordinator to discuss your perceptions of the team's emphasis in teaching and the limitations of your team's progress reports.

PROGRESS REPORT INQUIRIES

Progress reports have been distributed, and you are wearily leaving school as the intercom announces a phone call for you. Breathlessly arriving at the phone, you muster a "Hello" to which a volley of excited words respond. You assume the caller, who forgot to identify herself, is a parent of one of your students. Much to your amazement the children have arrived home already. In the flow of emotional words you decipher several questions: "How can Donna be doing 'good work' if she is 'not working up to her potential'? How can it be that she is doing well in Math and Science but poorly in Reading? Where on the report does it show how Donna is doing in comparison to the rest of her classmates? When Donna transfers to an East Coast school next year, how will this 'regular' school interpret this jibberish in terms of grade placement?"

Quickly it becomes obvious that if this parent attended your school informational meetings and read the explanatory insert of the progress report, she misunderstands or does not accept the philosophy of continuous progress. With a final comment that "a good teacher makes each child perform with the same competence as the next," Donna's mother is waiting for your response.

YOUR SOLUTION

YOUR REACTIONS TO THE ALTERNATE SOLUTIONS

ALTERNATE SOLUTIONS

1. Find out whether Donna's mother has attended school meetings or has read the progress report insert, and take it from there.
2. Suggest that if she is able and willing to come to school for a parent-teacher conference, you will be glad to explain Donna's progress and answer all her questions.
3. Answer her questions right away.

RECORD KEEPING OR RECORD CONFUSION?

Eager to share their progress with you in pupil-teacher conferences, these second-year pupils are enthusiastically engaged in their newly acquired independence in learning. As the year progresses, subsequent conferences reveal that you are the weakest link in providing a successful continuous progress program in Math. You memory is totally unreliable!

You have prepared a problem-solving packet for Michael that he completed satisfactorily "at least four weeks ago." Ann, who hasn't the pre-requisite skills to complete the task at hand, suggests, "This looks like work Marie has been working on." Indeed, it is Marie's! You draw a complete blank on your last conference with Marcia, so she patiently jogs your recollections. Although you know better, Helen insists that you told her to omit a skill packet on measurement, which is one of her weakest areas. Peter is distraught because "this period you were going to teach me how to use the abacus. Don't you remember you were going to borrow one for us to use?" Of course you were but the reminder comes a little late.

Obvious to all, your provisions for keeping records on the progress of thirty pupils need infinite improvement. Your move.

YOUR SOLUTION

YOUR REACTIONS TO THE ALTERNATE SOLUTIONS

ALTERNATE SOLUTIONS

1. Record your conferences on audio tape for review.
2. Have the pupils maintain records of their own progress.
3. Leave time between conferences and instruction to make notes about current achievements and objectives of the next conference.
4. Insist that your principal provide you with a paraprofessional.
5. Develop a checklist of items for conference use.

MEASURING STUDENT PROGRESS AND EVALUATING PROGRAMS

Educational measurement and evaluation are, psychologically and statistically, in sorry states! Learners continue to be victimized by parental and teacher misconceptions of the statistically derived grade level; their progress is periodically compared and misinterpreted with others of the same chronological age, in spite of their potential—background, personality, and self-concept. Teacher beliefs differ and become polarized about educational goals, their priority and assessment. Administrators continue to give teachers computer-scored printouts indicating only total percentiles and stanines in tested areas, while neglecting to return the standardized test booklets from which teachers could analyze the nature of student errors and design a program for student improvement. Parents, frequently reproached for pupil incompetence, discover a source of frustration in the report card they cannot interpret. Can there be any doubt why the public climate is ripe for recommendations of programs such as "performance contracting," "behavioral objectives," competency-based curriculum," and "accountability"?

There are critical needs that demand reform and revolution in the philosophy and practice of measurement and evaluation! If we continue in a style of bungling incompetence, industry will absorb our problems and deal with them as it has in Gary, Indiana and Texarkana. These decisions may not be ours for long unless some competent commitment and action are developed by educators. To complicate this situation, there are few substantial materials available and little in the line of teacher preparation to aid teachers in improving their fate.

Initially, decisions must be made with respect to what is worth teaching, how to provide effective instruction, and the most useful means of measuring student progress and evaluating learning programs. To date, the cognitive domain has monopolized curriculum and instruction, creating failures and "dropouts." This limited approach to educational goals has been, and will continue to be, inadequate until it is coupled with the affective domain, concentrating upon personal development, family living, citizenship, and occupational development. The cognitive and affective domains, in conjunction, create provisions for a digestion and integration of skills, attitudes, and concepts into a personal value system, satisfying a learner's needs while increasing his potential and affecting his total behavior.

Measurement and evaluation are not only culminating activities. They serve in diagnosing a pupil's strengths and weaknesses, in revealing through a pretest his prior knowledge and attitudes, and in providing essential feedback for the student about his progress and the teacher about the program assessment in light of the student's progress. This is a continuous cycle employing extensive varieties of student and teacher records, reporting devices, and interpersonal communication. Nowhere in educational measurement and evaluation is there a law requiring written tests as the only form of either. Teacher observations, questionnaires, and inventories, both written and verbal, are among the tools one might use, depending upon the purposes of the investigation. Philosophically this pattern of measurement and evaluation reflects a belief that since growth is personal, achievement must be assessed in terms of the individual's potential and progress. Furthermore, educational purposes and expectations should be realistically designed to correspond to a learner's potential and needs.

Contrary to the data available about learners and the learning process, conventional procedures for measurement and evaluation attempt to nullify individuality and threaten creativity. Apparent, too, is the assumption that motivation and anxiety are synonymous when, in operation, anxiety generally hinders learning. Most report cards and grading procedures indicate mediocrity for some, failure for others, and maximum achievement (can this be?) for a few. These systems only serve to reinforce the curriculum and behavior priorities held by teachers, in addition to demeaning the self-concepts of many children and parents. Whether grades take the form of A, B, C or partial scores of 100 percent nearly all assessments are subjective in nature. This subjectivity carries into the Mathematics program, which has for too long been referred to as an objective science. The idea that an answer is either right or wrong in Math isn't exactly applicable to $10 + 5 = ?$ The answer could be 15, but also $8 + 7$, $13 + 2$, or any other combinations of 15. A teacher makes a subjective decision in accepting or rejecting a student's answer!

Measurement has relied almost exclusively on standardized and teacher made tests for years, while little attention has been given to evaluating curriculum or to adjusting, improving, or discarding it. Infrequent adjustments have been made in instructional strategies. Rather than investigating and inspecting these items in terms of inadequacies, the *pupils* have been considered inadequate! Along with ability, achievement and personality tests come several severe problems encompassing test construction, administration, interpretation, and use of results. Although many instruments critically lack reliability and validity, many more are unsuitable for the population being assessed as emphatically illustrated in ghetto, bilingual, and rural communities. Standardized tests, administered simultaneously throughout the county or state, assume that learners should acquire the same skills and concepts by some magic date and do not account for variabilities in a student's health, emotional state, or physical aspects. Generally, all group standardized tests measure not what a child knows but how well he reads. It is pitiful to watch a child incapacitated by frustration, or perhaps poor reading skill, or perhaps time limitations, reach an emotional breaking point or produce low rating when you know from interacting with him that he knows and can apply the information being tested. Just what is really being measured and how seriously can the results be taken? Frequent references to group norms, in spite of their concealed inaccuracies and assumptions, create anxieties in children that may lead to cheating and teacher anxieties, which take forms such as "teaching for a test"!

Another problem arises with indiscriminate use of test results by unsophisticated interpreters. It is in this context that "dead-end" labels such as "slow learner" and "nonreader" emerge; such attitudes are not only detrimental to the student's future progress but are instrumental in shaping the efforts and approaches of his teacher. If instead a teacher were to look at what a child knows and what he needs to know, both the learner and teacher would make constructive progress and develop positive attitudes. All of the above assumes that what is being tested is important in the first place, which is highly debatable! All too often the purpose of measurement and what is actually being measured are not synonymous. More often than not, teacher-made tests are preferable, for the teacher has worked intimately with specific objectives and instruction with children; however, one of the major weaknesses of this kind of testing is the teacher's lack of skills in questioning and his ignorance about thought processes. For these reasons, tests constructed by a teacher typically aim at the lowest level of thought, namely recall. Instruction, too, seldom surpasses this! Yet another point to realize about all measurement instruments is the narrow range of objectives they provide. In developing a profile of the whole child, there is dire need to include information from every available source before conclusions are drawn and programs are established. Always keep an open mind, and remember that affective, psychomotor, and cognitive dimensions deserve your attention when measuring pupil progress and evaluating curricular and instructional decisions!

Accountability? Its impact and ramifications have only just begun to be felt in learning, teaching, measuring, and evaluating. Criteria of pupil progress and curricular and instructional revamping will help to keep the learner informed about his progress and demand that a teacher and learner both know the whys of where he is going and how he will recognize when he has arrived. Beware, however, the consequences of the potential misuses of accountability! If assembly-line conveyer belts, focused unilaterally on cognitive development, produce learners cast of a single mold as a finished product, even heaven won't be able to help us! Precautions must be taken to preserve and enhance the precious element of human variability among learners, and among teachers, for that matter. In formulating your position and competence in this aspect of teaching, contemplate the following: a teacher to all may be a teacher to none; a teacher to each, and learning's begun!

FOR FURTHER READING

ASCD. *Evaluation as Feedback and Guide.* Washington, D.C.: Association for Supervision and Curriculum Development, NEA, 1967.

Bloom, Benjamin, ed. *Taxonomy of Educational Objectives, Handbook I: Cognitive Domain.* New York: Longmans, Green and Co. 1956.

Holt, John. *How Children Fail.* New York: Pitman, 1964.

Krathwohl, David R., Benjamin S. Bloom, and B. B. Masia. *Taxonomy of Educational Objectives, Handbook II: Affective Domain.* New York: David McKay Co., 1964.

Marshall, Jon Clark. *Classroom Test Construction.* Reading, Mass.: Addison-Wesley, 1971.

Sanders, Norris M. *Classroom Questions: What Kinds?* New York: Harper & Row, 1966.

Storey, Arthur. *Measurement of Classroom Learning: Teacher Directed Assessment.* Palo Alto: Science Research Associates, 1970.

CHAPTER FIVE

Parent-Teacher Interactions

COCKTAIL-HOUR CAPTIVATOR

You are at a crowded cocktail party honoring new members of your husband's department. Even though you are saturated school, having taught days and prepared nights for parent conferences all this week, you find yourself gravitating toward the group of your friends who are listening to a newcomer expound upon his son's school.

"This school is really out of touch with the world! I don't want my son given 'success-oriented experiences' nor do I want him 'progressing at his own rate.' It's unhealthy for a child to grow up thinking he's in a personalized world where people help one another and are willing to wait for one to catch up with the others. It's the job of the school to insure experiences of failure and to teach kids how to cope with it in a dog-eat-dog fashion!"

"But," you ask, "isn't success the best way to teach them to cope with failure?"

"Young, lady, in my day no one took into account my experiences, needs, learning styles, or interests—no one spoonfed me and I've succeeded! I'd like to know how teachers can explain that! And besides, who are they kidding—with all those fancy words to camouflage teaching incompetence. Why just ask my boy what he does all day and he'll tell you he *plays* with his classmates. When I ask him what the teacher does he says she walks around and sometimes sits down to talk with two or three students. Today he started to build a rocket with two other boys. Now just what does that have to do with teaching him the Three R's?"

"If you're so upset, why don't you talk with his teacher?"

"Oh, that's right, parent conferences are the best way now. And they're so concerned with reporting 'pupil progress.' Report cards aren't explicit enough anymore. My son isn't *pro*gressing, he's being encouraged to *re*gress and *di*gress thanks to his teacher. Besides, we try to save our evenings for our family since we work all day. I'm not going to waste these precious hours talking with an incompetent about my son."

Finally, someone asks the inevitable, "Where does your son go to school?"

You are shocked to hear *your* school and *your* name in his answer; so are your startled friends! Your move.

YOUR SOLUTION

YOUR REACTIONS TO THE ALTERNATE SOLUTIONS

ALTERNATE SOLUTIONS

1. Identify yourself and proceed to tell the newcomer that he is an ignoramus whose attitude prohibits the possibility of his understanding educational philosophy in practice, so you will not waste your social hours or bore your listeners with a rebuttal.

2. Retort with a blow-by-blow accounting on each of the items he attacked and conclude by saying that you are his son's teacher.

3. Without revealing your identity, suggest that he always has the alternatives of transfering his son to a private school or moving his residence into a different school zone.

4. Call on your husband to defend your honor and competence.

5. Identify yourself and explain that he will be relieved to know that his son will have another teacher as of Monday morning, and leave the group before he has an opportunity to respond.

6. Dismiss the whole affair with a laugh, withdraw to find your husband's employer to give him a piece of your mind about his employment "folly."

7. Let the newcomer pick up the social void by identifying yourself without defending your teaching competence and see how he reacts.

YORK COLLEGE
PENNSYLVANIA

LIBRARY

83062

OUR GUINEA PIG HAS RICKETS!

Quite contrary to the usual admissions procedures, you wade through miles of red tape to acquire your thirty-second class member—an auburn colored, furry guinea pig! His classmates, after much contemplation, affectionately vote to name him "Rusty." His presence has been a rewarding experience for some pupils who, for the first time, have been motivated to follow directions, assume responsibility, and cooperate with each other while caring for Rusty. Most parents have cooperated by letting Rusty be a "weekend guest," and several have written or called to exclaim about the positive changes in their son's or daughter's behavior since his arrival.

One Monday morning Rusty returns to school with a note attached to his cage from his veterinarian hostess. Rusty has rickets, she declares, but you are not to be alarmed as the children cannot contract it from him. She prescribes an abundance of Vitamin D in his diet and speculates that this early diagnosis may save his life. Confiding that she has sworn her son to secrecy about Rusty's malady, she suggests that parents, without adequate information, may overreact by creating a raucus at the school and billing the school for the services of a fumigator.

Although this notion is presented in jest, you're sure there are a few parents who would at least consider these measures. You envision the next PTA meeting and being greeted by hostility.

How are you going to handle the situation with Rusty?

YOUR SOLUTION

YOUR REACTIONS TO THE ALTERNATE SOLUTIONS

ALTERNATE SOLUTIONS

1. Remove Rusty from your classroom, giving your pupils some explanation other than the real one.

2. Plan a health lesson about rickets, its prevention and cure. Incorporate the principles of scientific record-keeping to keep tabs on Rusty's condition.

3. Ask a team of pupils to research rickets and report their findings to the class.

4. Invite the veterinarian in to speak to your pupils and their parents.

5. Culminating a discussion about Rusty's condition and future, have the children write letters to their parents explaining the circumstances and their decision.

6. Take no action!

TRAUMA WITH AN AIDE

Jason, an eight-year-old, transfers into your class in mid-October. His mother escorts him to the room each morning. She always inquires about his academic and social progress or discusses her unfulfilled dream of becoming a teacher. Although you are interested, you are tired of beginning each day fifteen or twenty minutes late.

Careful observation of Jason's behaviors confirms your suspicions that he can't do anything by himself! He is dependent on you for direction and assistance at every step of a task, and he never ventures into anything new unless he is in a group with strong leadership.

The problem really develops the following week when Jason's mother is employed as a teacher's aide in your school and is assigned to your teaching team in spite of your vehement objections. Your teammates are upset because she spends nearly her entire time in your room.

Jason's peers accuse his mother of giving him correct answers and proofreading his papers before he gives them to you. Realizing that he has acquired speedy independence from you, you also begin to notice that whenever social problems erupt, Jason retreats to his mother for protection, which she eagerly provides.

One morning during a standardized reading test you discover Jason's mother, who insisted on helping you administer the test, is giving him the right answers. Action, you decide, is needed. How are you going to approach this situation?

YOUR SOLUTION

YOUR REACTIONS TO THE ALTERNATE SOLUTIONS

ALTERNATE SOLUTIONS

1. Insist that Jason's mother follow a schedule, designed by your entire teaching team, that equally divides her time among your team.

2. Have a heart-to-heart talk with Jason's mother about the academic, social, and psychological problems she is creating and make suggestions for solving them.

3. Threaten to submit your resignation to the principal unless he removes Jason's mother from your team.

4. Have Jason moved to another learning center, thus avoiding contact with his mother.

CONFERENCE OR CONFRONTATION?

As a black teacher in a newly integrated but predominantly white suburban school, you are experiencing the jitters of a first-year teacher approaching your first set of parent conferences. You scheduled Timothy's parents for your first conference because you're confident that you know him well; Tim thinks you're "absolutely groovy."

Upon their arrival, Timothy's parents survey the materials he uses daily, his folder of work you've gathered, and return to a circular table to proceed with the conference.

YOU: Timothy is such a vibrant, cooperative child . . .

MOTHER: He isn't at home and never has been. He's always hated school.

YOU: I believe he likes it this year. He's a good student in most areas and outstanding in Math. He gives such easy, accurate explanations; the children often understand his quicker than mine.

FATHER: Math has always been a major problem for Tim according to his previous teachers. Are you sure you're expecting enough from him?

MOTHER: Where did you do your college work?

YOU: I received my bachelor's degree from . . .

MOTHER: Are you fully certified to teach?

YOU: Not yet! I have to . . .

FATHER: You aren't?

YOU: No, I need a fifth year of college for permanent certification.

MOTHER: Do you live nearby?

YOU: No, I commute.

MOTHER: Oh dear, we have to meet our daughter's teacher and we're already late for that conference, but we wish we could stay longer with you.

FATHER: Yes, we'll talk with you again very soon.

What will you write on your conference report in the column "Conference Comments"?

YOUR SOLUTION

YOUR REACTIONS TO THE ALTERNATE SOLUTIONS

ALTERNATE SOLUTIONS

1. "Timothy's parents were more interested in my teaching credentials than in their son's progress. His father indicated a lack of confidence in my ability to diagnose Timothy's math ability. Very hostile!"

2. "Call Timothy's parents for a conference about *his* progress."

3. "I felt defensive answering Timothy's parents inquiries when I should have taken a positive attitude that they were genuinely interested in me and just making conversation. Have math tests and achievements available to substantiate conclusions!"

4. "Timothy's parents will be contacting me."

5. "It would have been advantageous to have met parents before parent conferences were scheduled!"

AN INVITATION TO DINNER

As Katherine greets you at the front door of her home, you recall her pride and excitement earlier today because she knew you were coming to dinner. She passes a tray of appetizers "I helped to make" and through her parents' conversation you realize they have quite an accurate picture of Katherine's school day in the new team-teaching organization. Katherine sure has done a fine piece of public relations, as her folks are pleased with what they've heard, or so it seems.

Throughout dinner you sense a strained relationship between Katherine and her parents, for every time Katherine offers an opinion or statement her mother interrogates her about the comment's truth and Katherine's honesty. "Are you positive? . . . You're exaggerating, aren't you? . . . Tell the truth now, please!" Each time Katherine sinks lower in her chair with her somewhat moist eyes cast downward.

Just as you are feeling definitely uncomfortable, Katherine's father explains that Katherine lives in her own world of fantasy and often is caught in the "chronic liar's problem of believing what she says." Katherine gives you an embarrassed glance as she excuses herself from the table. Her father immediately calls her back.

Silence engulfs the room as you search for something to do or say.

YOUR SOLUTION

YOUR REACTIONS TO THE ALTERNATE SOLUTIONS

ALTERNATE SOLUTIONS

1. Defend Katherine's perceptions, at least about conditions and experiences at school.

2. Tell her parents you've never had any reason not to trust Katherine's integrity.

3. Spill a glass of water hoping to relieve some of the tension and draw attention away from Katherine.

4. Inquire about her world of fantasy and ask for illustrations from it.

SHARING WITH PARENTS

Setting: Parent conference requested by a teacher. Both parents in attendance.

MOTHER: You've indicated that our son's reading problem is so severe that it is likely to impair his potential in school and drain any interest he has in learning. There must be something we can do at home in supporting your attempts here at school to alleviate or at least reduce this situation. Where do we begin?

TEACHER: Well now, neither of you have any preparation in teaching, human development, or remedial instruction. You certainly aren't very familiar with his learning habits and needs. Why don't you leave the education of your son in the hands of a professional? I just wanted you both to be aware of the problem.

Children belong to their parents! Most parents need to feel they can contribute something to their children's lives. Many parents express feelings of helplessness and absorb full blame for the failures their children encounter. Some, because of their own unhappy school days, fear talking with teachers, and others never question a teacher's decision because they have an awesome respect for teachers, whether or not it is earned. Still others tend to pressure their offspring toward unrealistic goals, which often influences learning and emotional strain. Yet there is room for all to assist their learners!

Teachers, fearing criticism and comparison, frequently contribute to the home-school communication gap by their lack of contact with parents unless something is dreadfully wrong. Sometimes they conceal themselves behind educational jargonese, thereby expanding the gap to a gulch! When a home-school conflict develops, a very confused child often develops anxieties disruptive to learning. If indeed we are teachers of children rather than of English or Social Studies, we dare not continue to exclude parents from education! Only a cooperative parent-teacher enterprise will ensure a comprehensive view of the whole child, who is then the real winner.

Involving parents in education will call for a good deal of sharing on many levels. First, they are most interested in whether you like their child. Formal and informal gatherings, parent conferences, field trips, community activities, PTA (or PEO) meetings and others will reveal your feelings. In discussions about their child, you will have opportunities to emphasize the importance of helping a child feel secure and loved, feel good about himself, strive to be independent, and cope with his world while acquiring self-control. Concrete suggestions for developing these aspects in a child must accompany these aims whenever needed. Your encouragement, sincere praise, and general support of parents will help them, and, in turn, their children.

At least since Sputnik, parents have been concerned about their offspring "learning a lot" in addition to the child's eagerness to learn. Shouldn't a parent's interest be expanded to include whether a child is creative, innovative, and responsive in new situations? In the near future, lives will not be shaped by work exclusively. Would it be advantageous for all to realize that the curriculum "frills" parents argue against might be just what is needed to maintain a healthy personality?

Do parents realize there are many ways to provide for learning? How many parents are convinced that a teacher-dominated classroom no longer reflects better learning procedures? Since parents prepare children with appropriate school behaviors, isn't it partially the school's responsibility to help keep parents well informed about educational changes?

Equally important to your success is your ability and capacity to listen. In a face-to-face situation, such as a parent conference, a sincere mutual exchange of information about the whole child and all aspects of his growth is communicated. You gain finer clarity and insight about this child as he vacilates between his worlds of home and school. Some innocently spoken piece of conversation may be a puzzle piece you or the parents have been missing. In this informal, relaxed exchange all parties begin to note common patterns in a child's attitudes, behaviors, and habits. Together you begin to problem solve and make decisions about the welfare of the child. Parents begin to realize the dynamic role they play in helping you to nurture their child's growth; so, too, do they begin to repair their "battered egos" as you begin to understand the problems faced by parents!

Enlarging upon these concepts, the entire community must be consistently informed and involved! Encouraged to contribute in decision making, parents and other members of the community should become familiar with a school's goals, philosophy, organization, innovations in curriculum and instruction, new materials, and old materials with new applications. The needs, resources, and attitudes of a community will greatly influence a school's emphasis, specific expectations, and budget. It is partially because schools have been isolated in their communities that so many school bonds and budgets have been defeated. Negotiating teams of teachers and administrators have settled for mediocre salary and teaching condition agreements with school boards, partially because these community members haven't seen first hand the value of education in our classrooms.

Among the many possibilities to reverse this trend, parent and community classroom volunteers are perhaps the most profitable. While involved in personal experiences with education today, they also are helping you to meet the needs of your learners by reducing your pupil-teacher ratio. There is so much more we could be doing for children if we'd only tap all of our resources. Also, frequent "informational meetings" and "open houses" are helpful in building community understanding. For instance, an informational meeting might explore the benefits of multi-age grouping one time, and a new Science curriculum another time. "Open house" might include children and their parents collectively investigating the learners' daily projects, materials, and media. It's great to listen to their marvelous explanations, to see their pride, and to watch Mom and Dad glow!

Accountability is a two-way street bridged by community-parent-teacher communication. Teachers might look into becoming expert salesmen—good talkers, doers, listeners, and evaluators. Conventionally a teacher's performance has been assessed by administrators, colleagues, and/or students. Could we be approaching a day when parents evaluate teachers? Are parents entitled? Are they qualified? Where will you stand?

FOR FURTHER READING

Cunningham, Luvern L. "Community Involvement in Change," *Educational Leadership,* 27 (January 1970): 363-366.

Dixon, Norman R. "The Home as Educative Agent," *Educational Leadership,* 25 (April 1968): 632-636.

Fantini, Mario D. *The Reform of Urban Schools.* Chaps. 3-6. Washington D.C.: Center for Study of Instruction, NEA, 1970.

Lurie, Ellen. *How to Change the Schools: A Parent's Action Handbook on How to Fight the System.* New York: Vintage Books, Random House, 1970.

Saylor, Mary Lou. *Parents: Active Partners in Education.* Washington, D.C.: American Assocation of Elementary-Kindergarten-Nursery Educators, 1971.

Smith, Mildred Beatty. *Home and School: Focus on Reading.* Glenview, Ill.: Scott, Foresman and Co., 1971.

CHAPTER SIX

Faculty-Administration Relationships

NOBODY CARES . . .

Beginning your career soon after Thanksgiving, you're the fourth teacher your second graders have had this year in this newly integrated ghetto school. Your welcome from the children—"No white bitch is learnin us!"—is reinforced by "Oh shit . . . we're not doing that!" in response to your first assignment.

Diagnosing several serious needs of your pupils, you seek the advice and assistance of district specialists, but your requests and eventual pleas are ignored. Revealing your frustrations to the grade-level chairman, you are cautioned not to "create waves."

The day of Parents' Night you encounter aggravation from the four most important people in your school life. The curriculum coordinator screams at you about your lack of discipline. On the way to lunch your group is reprimanded by the principal who commands, "Even though your teacher doesn't know any better, you children know you must maintain a single-file line in the halls!" The secretary is not speaking to you because you used the ditto machine and the custodian is perturbed because shades in the classroom are not left at even lengths nightly.

That night, your outlook brightens somewhat when you meet three sets of parents who praise your classroom efforts. Others you meet are polite but abrupt. The keynote speaker, grandfather of one of your knife-peddling students, swaggers a bit as he begins his speech on "Teachers." You wish that at least one other member of the teaching faculty had come tonight. Catching a glimpse of you, he discards the plurality of his topic to verbally attack your credentials. You hear him accuse you of mistreating children, stealing their possessions, and teaching them inaccurate information. The PTA ex-president comes to your rescue by suggesting that this is not of interest to the 600 parents who have gathered for tonight's program. Your community-minded principal continues to smile.

Returning home you decide your situation must be improved. What immediate action will you take?

YOUR SOLUTION

YOUR REACTIONS TO THE ALTERNATE SOLUTIONS

ALTERNATE SOLUTIONS

1. Since you met the district superintendent at a social affair, visit him to relate your perceptions of current events.

2. Either at school or individual homes, visit with parents to reveal your teaching qualifications and interest in their child. Share with them your plans and aspirations for each child.

3. Avoid any and all parent or faculty interactions while continuing to work constructively with pupils.

4. Phone the PTA ex-president to thank him for his support and to inquire about any community feedback he has received about you.

5. Contact the local representative of your teacher organization or union to have him bring charges of "incompetence" against your principal and colleagues.

CUSTODIAN CAPER

Early in the year you acquired a real appreciation for the importance of the custodian's role in your teaching. Not only did he replace your BB ridden window panes before the cold weather set in, but he also agreed to leave the furniture in your room the way you have it rather than forming rows with it nightly.

One afternoon in January you are getting the youngsters ready for physical education. Most of the girls, who must wear shorts for phys. ed., have "lost them," "left them at the bus stop," or "forgot this was a gym day." In a moment of sanity, several realize that they came to school wearing shorts under their skirts. Others search the lost-and-found box in the school office with success, but usually at least one pair is permanently missing.

Sneakers provide another story. Nearly every gym day one or a pair of them is added to your list of missing items. You set about writing gym excuses for the children without appropriate dress and hustle your class to the gymnasium. The children who are sidelined are obviously upset, as are their parents about duplicating gym attire.

On your way to the faculty lounge you meet Vernon, who had stayed behind to tie the laces on his sneaks. His wide eyes glow with excitement as he announces, "I'm going to be the class hero! Because I was late I cut through the boiler room, and do you know what I found? A gigantic pile of things including all those we have lost . . . and plenty more. Down at the bottom I found my old lunch bucket. Boy, is my Mom going to be mad! She just bought me a new Snoopy lunchbox!"

You send Vernon on to the gym after asking him to say nothing to the class until back in the classroom. As you head for the boiler room you wonder why your friendly custodian makes a habit of collecting things of children. In the boiler room, just as Vernon had described it, is the neatly stacked mountain of items but no custodian. What is your next move?

YOUR SOLUTION

YOUR REACTIONS TO THE ALTERNATE SOLUTIONS

ALTERNATE SOLUTIONS

1. Before the custodian returns, gather all the items you recognize and take them to your room.

2. Relate your discovery to other teachers and follow their lead.

3. Ask the custodian for an explanation.

4. Corral several students to help you deposit the custodian's collection into the school's lost-and-found box.

KEEP YOUR HANDS OFF ME!

Modly dressed, sufficiently lacking in the more traditional under-garments, and barefoot, your student teacher arrives at school, whereupon your principal promptly sends her home to don more "professional" clothing. Your intern does not reappear this day, and the second day she comes an hour late, stands in the doorway and introduces herself as Edna, "which means rejuvenation." You explain briefly that you'd like her to move into classroom involvement as quickly as possible. She gives no response, and yet as the day goes on she moves about the room helping a few youngsters. By the end of the week you are worried. Edna tenses whenever a child accidentally or intentionally touches her. "Keep your hands off me!" you overhear her tell the children. You discuss this problem with her, give suggestions, and eventually advise her to seek counseling facilities at the university, which she refuses to do. The problem intensifies.

Meanwhile, you are encouraged when Edna initiates a request to do a lesson in developing auditory and visual discrimination. You literally rave about her average lesson plan to give her confidence. As Edna begins her lesson you are amazed to discover that she has substituted hard rock records and psychedelic posters for her original ideas. Her fifteen-minute improvisation is anything but successful! When you inquire about the intended value of Edna's "lesson," she haughtily retorts that "the only way to teach a child to read is to let their souls be free." She concludes with the accusation that you obviously have "stifled the spontaneity, creativity, and free spirits of children."

Within no time you are meeting with your principal, Edna's college coordinator, and Edna. You share your perceptions until Edna interrupts: "You're running a baby sitting service, lady!" she cries as she departs with a flair. Because of your close contact with Edna, the other two parties feel it is your responsibility to make recommendations concerning Edna's future as a teacher. You are left with their assurance that they will support your opinions and the task of making a decision about Edna.

YOUR SOLUTION

YOUR REACTIONS TO THE ALTERNATE SOLUTIONS

ALTERNATE SOLUTIONS

1. State that Edna is an unsuitable candidate for an education degree and certificate.

2. Suggest that she be given a second chance to prove her ability in another ten-week internship with older children, but that she not complete her internship with you.

3. Recommend psychiatric counseling prior to completing her degree requirements.

4. Before writing an evaluation for the college ask Edna to come back to talk with you about her perceptions, for perhaps you *are* stifling your pupils' learning and creativity.

SUBSTITUTE FRUSTRATIONS

While student teaching you discovered the value of a substitute folder for times like this. Not well enough to teach one day, you notify the principal and convey the message that a folder of plans for the substitute is in the top drawer of your desk. You are confident that your children and sub will have a good day due to your careful preparation.

The following morning you return to your classroom to find havoc and chaos. Items on and in your desk are disorderly, games and materials are scattered everywhere, your paper closet reflects cyclonic activity, and your maps have been torn from their wall braces. Sure signs of vandalism! You immediately confer with your principal and she helps you restore order before the children arrive.

Composed and poised, you meet your eight, nine, and ten-year-olds, who rejoice in your return, filling your ear with tales of woe about "that lady" you sent to take your place yesterday. During reading you are shocked to learn that your substitute ordered your readers to *complete* their workbooks—those brand-new workbooks! Having received no assistance, your students dutifully followed directions and went ahead, scribbling and writing on every page! You try to eradicate your anger while helping the children erase their markings.

During the lunch period, you begin to check into other things—no attendance records were kept, your materials in the substitute folder are untouched although it is on the desk, and attached to it is a note:

Your class was the poorest disciplined group I've ever seen. Totally obnoxious, they talked all day long and never remained in their seats unless strongly scolded. I do wish you'd teach them some manners and in the future plan meticulously for your class in your absence.

How can you keep this from happening again?

YOUR SOLUTION

YOUR REACTIONS TO THE ALTERNATE SOLUTIONS

ALTERNATE SOLUTIONS

1. Identify who substituted for you and demand that her name be removed from the district's substitute list.

2. Discuss the situation with your pupils and explore ways to avoid these problems the next time you are absent.

3. Have a conference with the substitute and your principal to discuss the circumstances and conditions of your class and room.

4. Reprimand your class for their misconduct!

MRS. ALLEN'S CHOCOLATE CHIPS

Stopping by your neighbor's room to pick up an overhead projector, you are quickly introduced as the new (and only) male teacher who is "right next door to put straight anyone who misbehaves in this class." Having created this image for you, Mrs. Allen, as she escorts you to the door, exclaims, "It's really a shame you weren't teaching here last year when all of our children were beautiful products of professional families. What a disgusting contrast this year when our classes are spattered with chocolate chips—this 'experiment' in integration really depresses me!"

One glance around the room reveals the chocolate chips seated in the final two rows of the room. Mrs. Allen continues, "Why three of them tested out as my best readers, but knowing this couldn't be accurate, I placed them with the rest of their kind in my lowest group."

Standing with Mrs. Allen, you recall that your principal contended at your interview that you—a mod young bachelor from a liberal north-eastern background—would enjoy the challenge of wits his middle-aged "sewing circle" would provide. Was this what he meant? Is she serious, or is Mrs. Allen testing you?

Mrs. Allen, obviously amused by the length of your hair, is awaiting a reaction, as are her children who have heard the entire conversation!

YOUR SOLUTION

YOUR REACTIONS TO THE ALTERNATE SOLUTIONS

ALTERNATE SOLUTIONS

1. Abruptly leave the room before you lose your temper.

2. Ignore Mrs. Allen but tell her pupils that you are not the school ogre and that they are welcome in your room at any time.

3. Thank Mrs. Allen for the overhead projector and wave a "peace sign" to her pupils on your way out the door.

4. See your principal to inquire about Mrs. Allen's sincerity in her comments.

5. Call the local representative of the NAACP to have his staff investigate the racial inequalities of Mrs. Allen's classroom practices.

6. Joke with Mrs. Allen about the length of your hair and depart for your classroom.

A TIDY TENURE

This is your tenure year of teaching and a new principal, Mr. Conklin, has been assigned to your building. As promised in your initial faculty meeting, he has made frequent visitations to individual classrooms—"in an effort to get to know my staff." Each time he visits your room he notes with distaste its untidy and disorganized appearance. You have tried several times to engage him in conversation to explore your personal philosophy of education and each time it is promptly dismissed as "appropriate for the ivory tower" with no bearing on our (non) conversation.

With a PTA open house rapidly approaching, Mr. Conklin's visits occur more frequently. One morning you find yourself relieved of your teaching duties long enough to inspect classrooms he has identified as "suitable for effective teaching and learning to occur." You observe the even rows, cleared surfaces, immaculately organized cupboards and bookshelves, and well-modulated voices of teachers. Upon returning to your own duties you discover you have a meeting in the principal's office immediately after school.

As the children leave and you start to the meeting, you glance around the room. Particles of soil spilled while Sally and Jon planted seeds speckle the floor; partially mounted bulletin boards line one side of the room; the Math and Spelling program boxes covered with colorful contact paper litter one corner; newspapers, magazines, and paperbacks are stacked on the table in the Reading Center; the checker game has been left on the shelf to be resumed tomorrow; and chairs are everywhere. It was a productive day!

Arriving at your meeting, you detect displeasure in Mr. Conklin's nonverbal behavior. He begins by saying he has tried unsuccessfully to reach you in a tactful manner so now he'll come right to the point. Unless immediate changes are made in the appearance of your classroom, he will not recommend you for tenure and will request your resignation! He makes it quite clear he will not tolerate poor teaching in his building and no one could possible learn in the sloppy, chaotic environment you persist on maintaining. In conclusion, he feels he has done his very best to help you to become a good teacher, believing it is now up to you to exert some effort and take a personal pride in your classroom.

What is your response?

YOUR SOLUTION

YOUR REACTIONS TO THE ALTERNATE SOLUTIONS

ALTERNATE SOLUTIONS

1. Request a transfer or resign.

2. Promise that your room from now on will look just like the ones he is so proud of.

3. Call his bluff and proceed as usual.

4. Take your case to the district or county grievance committee, the NEA, AFT, or any other such mediator.

5. Visit your old principal to ask for his support and advice.

6. Ask him to spend a day with you in your "chaotic environment" and talk to your pupils about how much they may or may not be learning.

DEVELOPING PROFESSIONAL RELATIONSHIPS

Your development of satisfying, stimulating relationships with you colleagues and administrators is a critical aspect in becoming a teacher There are increasingly more opportunities in teaching that require greate cooperation and communication among your associates. Whether th setting is a self-contained classroom in which teachers are involved i cooperative teaching or formal team teaching, you will be a contributin member of a faculty. The successful operation of departmentalizatio depends upon the nature and degree of interpersonal relationships.

The changing nature of curriculum and instruction creates extensiv demands for continuous communication with specialized personnel: socia worker, psychologist, speech therapist, nurse, learning disabilities con sultant, librarian, music, art, and physical education personnel. In som school districts, administrators have attempted to gain maximal effective ness and availability of these resources by combining them into a "tas force," which upon your request will work with you over a schedule period of time.

The school's custodian, dietitian, and secretary will contribute to you resources and should be among the first people with whom you becom acquainted. The introduction of teacher aides, parent and communit volunteers presents another perspective in communication and coopera tion. Their roles may include developing instructional materials, supervis ing pupil activities, completing clerical tasks, acquiring supplies, an maintaining storage or resource areas, each of which is important to smooth operation.

The competence of the people above and the quality of your interactions will mold the complexities of your working climate. You will share inspirations, information, problems, opinions, advice, decisions, and feelings. As a new teacher, you will need their assistance and support in changing from group to individually paced activities, managing many different learning rates, levels, and styles, meeting pupil special skill needs, developing alternative learning experiences, and working in other problem-solving situations. They can help you acquire an understanding of the school philosophy, organization, and operation. Your success will be determined partially by your effectiveness and partially by the composition of the school's climate, which would be incomplete without the inclusion of administration.

Typically, a principal (or his assistants) is responsible for creating the organizational climate of a school. It is imperative that he be an effective teacher as well as a leader! He must inherently trust and value the uniqueness of each of his teachers and have a commitment to the belief that, when given the opportunity, teachers can solve their own problems, make their own decisions and policies, and improve their curriculum and instruction. Heresy? No! An effective principal is your best facilitator as he makes provisions for your teaching needs, establishes open lines of two-way communication between himself and his teachers, develops a democratic environment, helps you to clarify your own attitudes, values, and commitments, and provides instructional leadership. His beliefs about teaching and teachers are occasionally carried over into a teacher's beliefs about his students.

As in the case of any interpersonal relationship, communication is often the problem between a principal and his faculty. Communication can be both verbal and nonverbal, as revealed in the statements, "It's not what you say but how you say it!" and "Do as I say not as I do!" The credibility, appearance, voice, and delivery of the communicator influence a receiver. Interference with the message may come from physical and/or psychological "noise," such as a lawn mower outside or reflections on contradictory actions, respectively. You may hear the principal repeatedly say he is available to assist you, yet when you need him he is preoccupied with balancing budgets or assigning personnel. He may convey verbal commitment to trusting your students while not exhibiting trust in his teachers to use ditto, thermofax, or other machinery and equipment "because it is too expensive to repair if misused." It is as important for you to realize what you, as well as others, are communicating—verbally and visually! Your disposition and predispositions will influence your listening ability.

Teacher evaluation is a prominent concern among teachers. The best interests of both the school system and the teacher are served by a program of evaluation aimed at improvement. Similar to measurement of student performance and program evaluation, it should be a continuous process rather than a discrete event. While satisfying institutional needs, i should primarily encourage professional growth. Although the principal' major role is improving instruction, you are responsible for your professional growth, which might be promoted in a variety of ways, such as by video-tape analysis of your teaching behaviors, interaction analysis professional reading, visitations to other learning centers, attendance at national, state, and local conventions, and/or in-service and university study, just to mention a few.

Beyond the open classroom door are powerful influences on your growth and development as a professional. Professional organizations though their functions and periodicals may differ slightly, all exist for the betterment of learning and teaching. They are valuable resources for reviewing current research and exploring new ideas as well as exchanging points of view. You will have to become familiar with each in order to decide which memberships will best suit your needs and interests. Perhaps this is one of the first areas where you begin to individualize your own learning, and early investigation is wise, for most organizations have nominal membership fees for students. Otherwise, the second day of school you'll probably be asked to make some of these decisions in a blind confusion. At the national level the American Federation of Teachers and National Education Association will compete for your membership, in which case you will have to weigh their pros and cons in arriving at a decision.

In government, at all levels, you will gain glimpses of the total educational scene that will contribute to your personal growth and understanding of the profession. It will be beneficial to keep tabs on and take an active role in developments from the Department of Health Education, and Welfare and decisions passed along through the judicial system. As important as it is to know what issues NEA is lobbying for in Congress, you also need to be familiar with educational bills proposed by state legislators. The politics at the local level exist where teachers now enter into professional negotiations with the school board over working conditions, salary contracts, and fringe benefits. Considered here, too should be the mayor, city council, and other officials who make decisions that affect your professional life. It is extremely important for you to recognize all of these agencies and their potential influence on education

Education is unquestionably a cooperative endeavor. It involves your ability to know yourself, to communicate your feelings and ideas to others and comprehend theirs, and to work constructively and cooperatively with pupils, their parents, your colleagues, and administrators. Within this community you will grow in becoming a teacher.

FOR FURTHER READING

Combs, Arthur W. *The Professional Education of Teachers: A Perceptual View of Teacher Preparation.* Boston: Allyn and Bacon, 1965.

Heald, James E., and Samuel A. Moore II. *The Teacher and Administrator Relationships in School Systems.* New York: The Macmillan Co., 1968.

Jersild, Arthur T. *In Search of Self.* New York: Columbia University, 1952.

———. *When Teachers Face Themselves.* New York: Columbia University, 1968.

McNeil, John D. *Toward Accountable Teachers: Their Appraisal and Improvement.* New York: Holt, Rinehart and Winston, 1971.

Miles, Matthew B. *Learning to Work in Groups.* New York: Teachers College Press, 1967.

Moeller, Gerald, and David Mahan. *The Faculty Team: School Organization for Results.* Palo Alto: Science Research Associates, 1971.

Pharis, William L., Lloyd E. Robison, and John C. Walden. *Decision Making and Schools for the 70's.* Washington, D.C.: Center for the Study of Instruction, NEA, 1970.

Postman, Neil, and Charles Weingartner. *Teaching as a Subversive Activity.* New York: Delacorte Press, 1969.

Raths, Louis E., Merrill Harmin, and Sidney B. Simon. *Values and Teaching.* Columbus: Charles E. Merrill Books, 1966.

Sand, Ole. *On Staying Awake: Talks with Teachers.* Washington, D.C.: Center for the Study of Instruction, NEA, 1970.

Smith, B. Othanel, Saul B. Cohen, and Arthur Pearl. *Teachers for the Real World.* Washington, D.C.: The American Association of Colleges for Teacher Education, 1969.

Stinnett, T. M. *Teacher Dropout.* Itasca, Ill.: F. E. Peacock Publishers, 1970.

LB1555 .G53   010101 000
Giblin, Margaret Kelly.
Elementary school teaching: pr

‖‖‖‖‖‖‖‖‖‖‖‖‖‖‖‖‖‖‖‖‖‖‖‖‖‖‖‖

0 2002 0083483 2
YORK COLLEGE OF PENNSYLVANIA 17403

83062

LB
1555   GIBLIN
.G53   ELEMENTARY SCHOOL
            TEACHING: PROBLEMS...

DISCARDED

LIBRARY

5